It's My Life Now

Now in its third edition, *It's My Life Now* is a guide for survivors who have left an abusive relationship. It addresses—in clear, non-threatening language—various issues associated with abuse and violence, including post-relationship emotions, psychological impact, dealing with children, personal safety, legal problems, and financial security. Each chapter dismantles common myths about being in and leaving an abusive relationship and contains activities for self-exploration that survivors can complete as they navigate a new life free from abuse. Recommended by the National Coalition of Domestic Violence, this book is designed to benefit any survivor, no matter how much time has passed.

Meg Kennedy Dugan, MA, is the executive director of Voices Against Violence, a crisis center in Plymouth, New Hampshire. She serves on the local SART (Sexual Assault Resource Team) and is on the executive committee of the New Hampshire Violence Against Women Campus Consortium. For the past 17 years, she has worked with survivors of domestic and sexual violence and stalking.

Roger R. Hock, PhD, is professor of psychology and human sexuality at Mendocino College in Northern California. He is the author of *Forty Studies that Changed Psychology: Explorations into the History of Psychological Research, 7th Edition* (2012, Pearson) and *Human Sexuality, 5th Edition* (2016, Pearson). He received his PhD from the University of California at San Diego.

It's My Life Now

THIRD EDITION

Starting Over After an

Abusive Relationship

Meg Kennedy Dugan & Roger R. Hock

Routledge
Taylor & Francis Group

NEW YORK AND LONDON

Third edition published 2018
by Routledge
711 Third Avenue, New York, NY 10017

and by Routledge
2 Park Square, Milton Park, Abingdon, Oxon, OX14 4RN

Routledge is an imprint of the Taylor & Francis Group, an informa business

© 2018 Meg Kennedy Dugan and Roger R. Hock

First edition published by Routledge 2000
Second edition published by Routledge 2006

Library of Congress Cataloging-in-Publication Data
A catalog record has been requested for this book

ISBN: 978-0-415-41518-7 (hbk)
ISBN: 978-0-415-41519-4 (pbk)
ISBN: 978-1-315-18164-6 (ebk)

Typeset in Sabon
by Wearset Ltd, Boldon, Tyne and Wear

Contents

Acknowledgments

Meg and Roger would like to express their sincere thanks to Anna Moore for her encouragement and support for this third edition of *It's My Life Now*. They also send all their best wishes out to those courageous survivors who have freed themselves from an abusive and/or violent relationship and are rebuilding a life free from fear and pain.

Meg would also like to thank her mother, Helen C. Kennedy, who continues to be a source of inspiration and guidance. Her lifelong dedication to social equity, as well as reverence for all life, have impacted all who know her. In addition, Meg wishes to acknowledge Tina, Tina E., and Sonja, all of whom for the past five years have shared with her their knowledge, passion, and insight into the understanding of survivors of domestic abuse. They have positively affected thousands of lives by helping those individuals know that they have options, are believed, and support is available.

Introduction

Welcome to the third edition of *It's My Life Now: Starting Over After an Abusive Relationship*.

This edition, in addition to ensuring that readers who are survivors feel in charge of their own decisions and direction in life, helps to rebuild their self-esteem, thereby finding one more way to leave behind some of the remnants of the abuse they had to endure. From the publication of the first edition in 2000, through the second edition published in 2006, to the present, *It's My Life Now* has been helping to guide those who have managed to leave an abusive relationship into and through their crucial transition to a new life, a life free of abuse, violence, and fear. In this third edition we continue to provide this guidance, adding new, valuable insights and strategies, and updating chapters to reflect the latest approaches to recovering and rebuilding a life after abuse. This new edition also expands upon our discussion of the creation of and effects of post-traumatic stress disorder (PTSD) in survivors.

This can be an exciting time for you; yet, as you know, it is also a period of adjustment, insecurity, anger, confusion, self-doubt, and, at times a scary reentry into a new world. These feelings may emerge immediately after the relationship, or they may take months or years to surface.

Most books, articles, and other media about domestic violence focus on the abusive relationship itself: how to know if you are in one, why people stay in violent relationships, why you should leave, how to get out, and so on. Rarely is adequate consideration given to what many see as one of the most critical times for a survivor of an abusive relationship: the time after you leave.

Not all abuse is caused by men in heterosexual relationships. Unfortunately, women abuse men and same-gender abuse occurs in gay and lesbian relationships, as we discuss in Chapter 6, "Abuse of Men by Women, and Abuse in Gay, Lesbian, and Transgender Relationships." However, abuse by men against women is the most common form of relationship violence. Consequently, this book is written using female pronouns and discussing at length issues that particularly apply to women as victims and survivors. This in no way negates the horror of abuse in other types of partnerships. *Anyone* who has suffered from relationship abuse and domestic violence will find information throughout this book relevant and helpful.

Those who have never experienced an abusive or violent relationship often believe that once survivors find their way out, all difficulties are solved: life is good, they are safe, and recovery will be swift. But survivors know leaving is not the end of the nightmare. It is the beginning of a difficult, yet fulfilling and rewarding journey toward healing and happiness. This book can serve as your guide.

We have divided the book into three time frames that are relevant to the healing process for survivors of abuse: *Looking Back* (Chapters 1 to 6), *Now* (Chapters 7 to 11), and *Looking Forward* (Chapters 12 to 17).

As you look back on your unhealthy relationship, your first step toward healing is acknowledging to yourself that you have, indeed, survived an abusive relationship. You may have no doubt that you were in an abusive or violent relationship. On the other hand, you may be hesitant to define your relationship in those terms. Now that you are out, feelings may be surfacing telling you your relationship was much worse than "just difficult." Chapter 1 assists you in reviewing the characteristics and behaviors of abusive relationships. It will help clarify the nature of your relationship and help you move forward.

The next step in your journey is ensuring your safety. As survivors of violent relationships know, abusers can be just as dangerous or pose an even greater threat after the relationship ends. Chapter 2 offers some guidelines for maximizing your level of personal safety. This is a crucial component in your process of emotional healing.

Loss of self-esteem is one of the first and most pervasive effects of abuse. A major part of being able to take complete control over another's life is to make her feel weak and worthless. Chapter 3 provides several Self-Exploration exercises designed to help survivors recognize their value and self-worth and regain their self-esteem.

Chapter 4 addresses the "hidden horror" of sexual violence in abusive relationships. Healing from your relationship is even more difficult if it included sexual abuse. Many survivors may not recognize or acknowledge they have been sexually abused by their partners. Rape and other forms of sexual abuse are emotionally devastating experiences. If sexual abuse was part of the violence you experienced, you may feel an extra layer of pain and distress. You can get past this too, but some additional steps may be necessary.

Your current challenges begin with Chapter 5's discussion of a confusing and often painful obstacle in your healing process: lingering feelings of love for your ex-partner. How is this possible? He's violent. He has abused you. Shouldn't this knowledge destroy any feelings of love or affection you may have once felt for him? Human emotions are not always "clean" and logical. In reality, many survivors of abusive and violent relationships continue to feel love for their partner after leaving. Discovering why you have these feelings and what they mean will empower you to move beyond them.

The possibility of abuse and violence exists in all intimate relationships. Chapter 6 focuses on those of you who do not fall into the traditional abusive-relationship roles of female as victim, male as abuser. This includes female-on-male abuse and abuse in same-sex relationships. For you, surviving and escaping your abusive partner, as well as recovering and regaining your life after leaving, often involves unique and sometimes even more difficult hurdles than those faced by survivors of the more typical male-on-female abusive relationships.

You may also notice you are experiencing a sense of loss and grief. These feelings are a normal part of losing any intimate relationship, even one that was painful and destructive. Relationships are complex, and, in some ways, violent ones are even more complex than healthy ones. Chapter 7 focuses on how the sense of loss you experience after an abusive relationship ends can, ironically, feel as distressing as losing a healthy relationship.

Now that you are out and in relative safety, you will begin to feel emotions that were not possible to feel when your main focus was survival. It is very common for survivors to experience intense anger, depression, and guilt after leaving an abusive relationship. Again, these feelings can be very uncomfortable and may be more difficult to work through than you expected. Nevertheless, they are a normal part of this painful transition. They are part of allowing yourself to feel again. Chapter 8 will guide you through emotions that may feel too strong and will help you regain those you have lost. Healthy emotional functioning is an important turning point on your path to recovery.

So, how much healing remains for you? What are some indicators that you still have work to do in your healing process? Chapter 9 will help you take a step back and consider some emotional and behavioral signposts along your path to healing. How are you feeling about yourself? How are you interacting with others? How are you functioning on a day-to-day and even hourly basis? What activities are you becoming involved in? Being attentive to these thoughts and actions can help reassure you that the healing process has begun.

Sometimes, survivors need to consider other important people in their lives as they are healing. Chapter 10 focuses on children who may have been part of your abusive relationship. Most likely, they were victims too, either directly as the recipients of abuse, or indirectly as they observed the terrible events occurring in their home. Now they need support from you and protection from the violent ex-partner. You need to help them cope with what has happened. Dealing with the effects of the abuse in your children's lives can be complicated and emotional.

After you leave a violent relationship, you hope your friends, family, and coworkers can offer the support you so desperately need. Unfortunately, this is not always the case. Many people are so uncomfortable with the idea of relationship abuse that they retreat from it and from you. Others may not accept or understand what you have been through or even blame *you*. Part of your healing process is deciding which people to allow into your life. In addition, you need to be prepared to deal with those who withdraw from you, disappoint you, or are unable to offer the support you thought you could count on. Chapter 11 explores the difficult process of dealing with the reactions of others in your life.

Although healing your psychological and emotional wounds is your chief concern, you may find many external, practical matters feel equally pressing as you begin to *look forward* toward a happier future. In the aftermath of an abusive relationship, many women must face difficult and often complex legal and financial challenges. These may include child custody and visitation arrangements, divorce proceedings, property and support disputes, and credit hassles, to name a few. Chapter 12 discusses the practical considerations you may be facing and offers guidance in finding the professional assistance you may need. Handling these issues effectively will help keep them from interfering with your healing.

What specific steps should you take toward emotional healing? Chapter 13 focuses on three of the most incapacitating emotions most domestic violence survivors face: anger, depression, and anxiety. It is important for you to recognize these feelings, assess the extent to which they may be affecting you, and take the appropriate actions to address them. You may find that you are perfectly capable of dealing with your intense emotions on your own. However, many survivors whose emotions begin to interfere with healing and moving on with their lives find that their healing process benefits greatly from the guidance of a trained professional counselor.

A major casualty of abuse is self-esteem. Many survivors judge themselves unworthy of love and respect. Rebuilding self-esteem begins with careful assessment of who you are now and whom you want to become. Chapter 14 will assist you in examining your feelings and perceptions about yourself. As you begin to reestablish a positive self-concept, you will realize you deserve much more from a partner. You deserve to be treated with respect and kindness. It's not about finding a perfect, fairy-tale life. It is about knowing what you can and should expect from an intimate relationship and making sure that you get it.

For some survivors, one of the most confusing issues following an abusive relationship is the temptation to return to her abuser. Your ex-partner wants you to come back. He is probably saying all the right things about how he has changed, how sorry he is, how it will never happen again. He sounds so convincing! In fact, you may have left him in the past, only to return to watch the tension build and the abuse and violence begin again. Your friends and relatives are stunned, anxious, and disbelieving when you mention you are thinking of going back to him. Chapter 15 examines the reasons you may be tempted at times to return to him. It also helps remind you of why you left. Making the right decision about returning to an abusive partner is a crucial step in regaining control over your life.

One of the most complicated and painful situations in the aftermath of an abusive relationship is an ex-partner who is still in your life. If you had children together, you may have contacts with him, either in person or indirectly through your children. If you live in the same community, you may run into your abuser now and then in any number of circumstances. Chapter 16 will help you anticipate these contacts, maintain your safety, and protect you from further pain and abuse.

Can you ever love again? The answer is yes! However, a destructive relationship usually leaves the survivor with the very real fear of repeating the cycle. Healing from the abuse and moving on involve recognizing and avoiding potentially unhealthy relationships. Finding love again as a survivor of relationship abuse or domestic violence is the theme of the Chapter 17.

You are not alone. Many others have survived abuse and violence and regained their lives. Because abusive relationships are so terribly common, many sources of help and information are available to you as you travel along your difficult post-relationship path. The section at the end of the book called "Resources" offers Internet sites, and telephone hotlines to assist you in finding the support you may want and need.

Your new life may seem frightening, confusing, and overwhelming right now, but you are probably farther along the path to healing than you think. It *is* possible to believe in yourself, have a healthy, intimate relationship, and be happy. Although the road may seem long and your destination may not be in sight quite yet, it exists. It is just around the corner.

Caution: As you are reading this book, you may find an increase in intensity of certain symptoms resulting from your experience of abuse. Additionally, you may sense the appearance of new uncomfortable symptoms. These are signs that healing is taking place. However, if, as you read through these chapters and work on the Self-Exploration exercises, you begin to feel more depressed, anxious, or angry, or if you begin to question your control over your emotions, you may need to consider obtaining professional counseling to help you take full advantage of this book and begin to move forward in your life.

You should also be aware that parts of this book may be more difficult for some of you than for others. Many survivors, as the result of the abuse, may find their ability to gauge their own and others' emotions and actions correctly. Many survivors require a somewhat longer time period to process information; their memory may be a bit impaired temporarily; and they may have difficulty reading when people are angry, sad, or otherwise distressed. In addition, some survivors experience a period of numbness that feels as though they out of touch with their own emotions.

If you find these issues are preventing you from working on your healing process, you may want to some time to calm your troubling emotions before setting out on your journey through this book. Some very basic techniques may help with this, including: creating a more structured and predictable routine for yourself; relaxation and breathing techniques; going for walks or other mild physical exercise; or working to "slow down" a bit in your day-to-day, minute-to-minute life. For example: Here's one technique that many people find helpful when they feel that life or their emotions are become overwhelming. It's called "progressive muscle relaxation."

Progressive Muscle Relaxation (PMR) is a proven technique for reducing tension in your body. PMR involves tensing and relaxing muscle groups throughout your body, one group at a time. It can be particularly helpful if you store stress in your body. It is also especially helpful when you are having difficulty falling asleep at night. It's best if you can listen to the following instructions while you are relaxing, so you might want to record this or have a friend read it to you (or if you are using an e-reader, you may be able to activate the narration feature for this exercise).

Sit in a comfortable chair or lie on the floor or a bed. Begin the process by tensing your right foot and holding that tension for a slow count of five. Then release the tension in your foot and completely relax it for another count of five. Next, tense the muscles of your right ankle for a count of five and relax it for a count of five. Now tense, then release, your right calf muscles in the same way. After your finish tensing and relaxing all the muscles in your right leg, move onto your left foot and leg. Slowly continue this progressive tensing and releasing of individual muscle groups until you have covered your entire body from your toes to your scalp. The chart below will guide you through all your muscle groups in the recommended sequence.

Be sure to include all of the following areas when performing PMR techniques. For each muscle group, remember to tense and relax for a count of five each.

- Right foot
- Right ankle
- Right calf
- Right thigh
- Left foot
- Left ankle
- Left calf
- Left thigh
- Buttocks
- Back
- Stomach
- Chest
- Right hand
- Right wrist
- Right forearm
- Right biceps
- Left hand
- Left wrist
- Left forearm
- Left biceps
- Shoulders
- Neck
- Face
- Jaw
- Tongue
- Forehead
- Scalp

Be sure to include every muscle group. Do not rush through the process by tightening your entire leg or arm. Take each individual part separately. For example, tense and release your hand, then your wrist, then your forearm, and then your biceps.

Try PMR for a few weeks. As with all relaxation techniques, it might take a while to learn to relax completely. If unwanted thoughts enter your mind as you are going through the process, gently push them out and focus on your body. Do not become angry or upset if you lose your focus. It takes time, but once you are skilled at PMR, it can be a great weapon against stress.

We hope that this new edition of *It's My Life Now* will help survivors understand that they were not to blame for the abuse. It is also hoped that this book will help you to move on to a new life free from abuse, one where you can believe in yourself and all your wonderful qualities and traits.

Meg Kennedy Dugan
Roger R. Hock

Where Will You Be in Five Years?

A helpful way to assess your perception of the future is to imagine in some detail where your life will be in five years. The following exercise will help you consider your goals and your belief in your ability to obtain them. Describe as much as you can about your life five years from now in each of the following categories.

Note: The time needed to heal varies from person to person. Many of the exercises in this book suggest that you repeat them in one month. However, you should feel free to extend that interval to six weeks, two months, or even six months if it better fits your personal pace of healing. It is also perfectly appropriate to repeat the exercises more than once if you wish.

Job or Career_____

_____

_____

_____

_____

Intimate Relationship_____

_____

_____

_____

_____

Family Life_____

_____

_____

_____

_____

Friendships_____

_____

_____

_____

_____

Physical Appearance_____

_____

_____

_____

_____

Other Issues that Apply to You Personally

1. _____

_____

2. _____

_____

3. _____

_____

Now that you have finished describing your perceived future, spend some time reviewing it. How does it make you feel? Do you feel happy and enthusiastic about the future you envision? If you do, that's great! You are on the right track. On the other hand, if you feel discouraged by your view of where your life is going, you need to work on starting over and healing from the abuse. *We recommend that you repeat this exercise in about a month and periodically throughout your healing process.* Comparing your answers over time will allow you to see changes and progress in your views about yourself, your life, and your healing.

PART

I

Looking Back

1

Were You in an Abusive Relationship?

Myth: You must have done something to cause the abuse.

Myth: Abuse only happens to people who are weak.

Myth: Victims who don't leave an abusive relationship right away must have something wrong with them.

Many explanations exist for the components of intimate partner abuse. Every intimate relationship is unique and each abusive intimate relationship is unique, too. However, as you look back on your relationship, you will discover certain signs, clues, and characteristics that should help you decide if yours was an abusive relationship. Two significant indicators are common to virtually all cases of relationship abuse: *power and control.*

Defining Abuse

Relationship abuse usually involves a *pattern* of abusive events. Except in rare cases, a single incident usually does not constitute abuse. Instead, victims experience a repetitive pattern of controlling behaviors that typically does not stop and escalates over time.

Abusive relationships are based on *power* and *control*. The abuser's goal is to exert power over you to ensure that he is in complete control of you and of the relationship. Your partner's controlling tactics may have been subtle and not easily recognized. He may have tried to convince you that controlling your time, the friends you have, and most or all of your daily activities was a sign of caring or wanting only the best for you. As time went by, however, the control you once had over your life disappeared. Gradually, using a wide range of strategies, he was able to render you powerless and place himself in control of you and the entire relationship.

Although all abusive relationships share the characteristics of power and control, the specific behaviors used by abusers to achieve their goals vary greatly. At the beginning of your relationship, you may not have even noticed the negative behaviors. You may have felt that some of the behaviors seemed loving and attentive. Your partner might have been so jealous of your time that it seemed extreme, but he convinced you it was because of how much he loved you. He was probably with you almost all the time and told you that he couldn't stand to be without you. He seemed to put you on a pedestal, which probably felt wonderful. The relationship grew very quickly and when you were not together, he called or texted you a lot. You may have thought at the time that this was the best relationship of your life.

Slowly, however, some of those wonderful things began to change. Perhaps you felt as if your partner wanted to move ahead in the relationship *too* quickly. He may have pressured you into spending all your time together to the exclusion of other friends and family members. After the times you were apart, he constantly asked where you had been and what you had been doing. Sometimes this questioning may have erupted into outbursts of anger and jealousy.

Next, you may have noticed that your abuser was becoming more critical of you. The criticism may have been about whom you went out with, the way you dressed, how you talked, or even the music you liked. Each time, he followed the criticism by saying he was only telling you these things to "help you." And each time he once again professed his deep love for you.

At this point, you may have grown a bit concerned, but probably passed it off as some sort of stress your abuser was under. He apologized for the jealous outbursts and *promised* it would never happen again. He convinced you not to worry. But as the criticism continued, you may also have begun to feel critical of yourself and your own activities as well.

Slowly, you began to realize that the troubling behavior was not going away: it was getting worse, it was becoming abusive. Still, even as this negative behavior increased, you might not have recognized it as abuse. You may not have liked what he did or said to you; you may have felt hurt and unhappy, but he convinced you it was a "normal" part of a relationship, a problem that the two of you could work out somehow. Or he convinced you that you were somehow to blame and if you could just change, his behavior toward you would change as well.

As the relationship continued, you probably read or heard stories about intimate partner abuse, relationship abuse, or domestic violence. These were horrific stories where a victim was murdered by an intimate partner or a victim whose partner's violence sent her repeatedly to the emergency room. These overtly physically violent examples of abuse may have made it even more difficult for you to label what was happening in your relationship as abuse because it was not the same, not so outwardly violent. Abuse in your own life may have taken forms that were initially much less obvious. Whether or not you experienced physical abuse, you may have been the victim of verbal, emotional, sexual, or spiritual abuse. You may have never experienced any physical violence at all and yet you survived an extremely abusive relationship.

If you were the victim of abuse in childhood or in an earlier relationship, the process of recognizing the abuse may have been a bit different. If all you had ever known were abusive relationships, your abuser might have used this knowledge to make it more difficult for you to recognize a problem existed. If you had been abused in previous relationships, you may have hoped this one would be better, but you may not have realized what constituted a healthy, non-abusive relationship.

Because of what your past abusers told you, you may have believed you were just overreacting. Your abuser may have used his knowledge of your past abuse to minimize the seriousness of his own abusive behaviors. He may have pointed out all the "nice" things he did for you and how you were imagining these problems because you were "oversensitive." You may have taken a long time to realize that this was indeed abuse, that it was wrong, and that you deserved better.

Because the abuse or violence may come and go, and the relationship alternates between terrible, abusive times and better or even good times, an abuser can use this back-and-forth to make you unsure and question whether you have an unhealthy relationship and a violent partner.

The Power and Control Wheel

One reason you may have found it difficult to identify what you experienced as abuse is the *myth* that only overt violence constitutes abuse. In reality, there are a multitude of means and tactics for exerting power and control in a relationship. Often survivors don't recognize the abuse in their relationships because they have been exposed to a list of the various means abusers use to exert power and control over their victims. The Duluth Domestic Violence Power and Control Wheel may help you identify the multitude of ways he abused you.

In your abusive relationship you may have found that there were times when the abuse was not as obvious or overt. There may have been times of outward calm when no visible abuse was happening. You probably recognized this was a way your abuser found to keep you unsettled by alternating outward emotional, verbal, or physical abuse with times of compliments and quiet. A way to visualize this is to think of a roller coaster. During the "highs" you might have felt more able to move about your daily life while still having that inward dread of what was to come. Many victims talk about this period of "calm" as the worst times not knowing when the other shoe would drop. At times that freefall into violence occurred leaving you not knowing where it would end. Other times the "waiting" seems interminable. Once over, you had no way of knowing what would come next. Your abuser's goal was to keep you off balance, unsure of him or yourself.

Figure 1.1 Power and Control Wheel

(Reprinted with permission of Domestic Abuse Intervention Programs [DAIP]).

Figure 1.2 The Rollercoaster of Abuse.

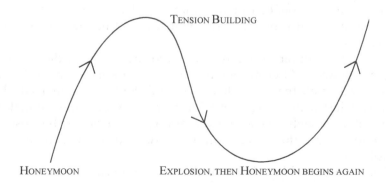

Emotional Abuse

If you are like many people who have survived an abusive relationship, you may find that, paradoxically, the physical abuse feels
somehow less damaging in the long run than the emotional abuse
you endured. Emotional abuse is so insidious and psychologically
devastating that it can take the longest time to heal. Bruises, cuts, or
even broken bones often mend faster than the wounds of emotional
abuse. And your abuser probably used many strategies to take
control of and manipulate your feelings and emotions.

Did your abuser make you feel unworthy of love? Did he work to
convince you that you were stupid, ugly, or fat? Through these
tactics, he persuaded you that no one would ever find someone like
you attractive. By doing this, he was working to guarantee that you
would stay with him.

Did your abuser make you feel that the abuse was all your fault?
He probably tried to make you believe that something must be
wrong with you because otherwise the abuse would stop. You came
to hope and believe that if you were only more patient, better organized, a better lover, or somehow different, the abuse would stop. But
no matter what you did, the abuse continued. You slowly began to
feel worthless, hopeless, and helpless.

After each incident of abuse, your abuser probably tried to make
it seem as though you caused it. It may have gone something like
this: "I'm so sorry *but* if only you hadn't..." This created a way for
him to seem repentant while, at the same time, telling you it was all
your fault.

Your abuser may have threatened you if you didn't do exactly
what he wanted. Threats can be a devastating form of emotional
abuse. Sometimes an abuser's threats are overt and clear: "The next
time I see you talking to him, I'll fix it so you'll never talk again."
Other threats, though, can be more veiled and subtle: "Sure, go
ahead and go out tonight. I hope your cat will be OK while you're
gone."

Also, your abuser probably minimized the extent of the abuse in
numerous ways. After an emotional assault he may have told you
that it wasn't all that bad, that you didn't look very damaged, that
you were just being a big baby. This tactic had the power of making
you feel as though you were exaggerating the incident, but also let
you know that if this wasn't "all that bad," much worse things were
possible.

Here is a partial list of actions that constitute emotional abuse:

- Entitlement ("I have a right to sex"; "I expect you to do what I say.")
- Withholding ("I don't need to tell you what I'm thinking or feeling"; "Why would I want to make love with someone like you?")
- Emotionally misrepresenting ("You're not hurt, what a joke. You're just being too sensitive.")
- Not taking care of himself (doing drugs, engaging in high-risk behaviors such as driving recklessly, not seeking medical care, not bathing)
- Withholding help (with money, chores, childcare)
- Acting out excessive jealousy ("Why were you talking to him? You want to be with him instead of me? You've been cheating on me, haven't you?")
- Threatening self-injury or suicide ("If you leave me, I'll kill myself, you can count on it—and it'll be on you.")
- Threatening to hurt or kill you, your friends, relatives, or pets ("You like your little friend so much? It would be awful if something happened to her when you went to the store.")
- Controlling you (taking control of where you go, whom you see, what you do, all the decisions in your life, both the life you shared and your own life)

Refer back to the Power and Control Wheel for more examples of Emotional Abuse.

Verbal Abuse

Your partner may have abused you with *words* rather than, or in addition to, physical or emotional violence. Attacks of verbal abuse may have been directed at you face-to-face, or might have been in the form of negative, degrading comments about you to others, or in texts or emails. Your partner may have belittled and humiliated you in front of others or suggested to others that you were being unfaithful to him, even though this was not true.

Verbal abuse can be extremely painful, and its damaging effects long lasting. As with physical violence, verbal abuse can take many different forms, but the result was to change your view of yourself. It may have been designed to make you feel afraid and powerless. It may have focused on making you feel worthless and somehow to blame for what your ex was doing to you. It may have also been intended to convince you that you were small, unworthy, unattractive, stupid, insensitive, and so on, and that no one but him would ever love you (see previous section, "Emotional Abuse").

Here is just a partial list of behaviors that are included in verbal abuse:

- Yelling at you
- Ridiculing you
- Accusing you
- Blaming you
- Being sarcastic to you
- Disparaging your ideas
- Threatening you
- Calling you names
- Insulting you
- Belittling you
- Rejecting your opinions
- Intimidating you
- Criticizing you
- Humiliating you
- Mocking you
- Putting you down
- Trivializing your needs and desires

Spiritual Abuse

Your abuser may have found ways to exert control over you by exploiting and criticizing ideas that are sacred to you: your spirituality, your personal values, your morals, and your philosophical beliefs. Did he ever try to use religious writings to convince you that his abusive actions were OK? He may have quoted passages from your religion's sacred writings or your valued philosophical texts and interpreted them to imply that you were his property; that you were supposed to abide by his needs, and submit to his authority and power; that if you disobeyed, you should be punished. No matter what spiritual convictions you hold precious, your abuser may have attempted to minimize them, thereby minimizing you.

In addition to using your religious beliefs against you, your abuser may have denigrated nonreligious principles that are sacred to you. These are beliefs that may be an integral part of your upbringing and a solid part of who you are. Your convictions about your relationship to other people, to animals, or to the environment are a few of the beliefs that may have been fodder for his abuse.

Here are some examples of spiritual abuse:

- Trivializing your ideas, opinions, views, and desires
- Discrediting your values as unimportant, silly, or unrealistic
- Stating that his beliefs are the only "right" beliefs
- Using sacred texts to justify the abuse
- Using religion to justify the controlling behaviors
- Denying your religious beliefs

- Preventing you from attending religious services or participating in sacred ceremonies
- Preventing you from observing holy days and rituals
- Ridiculing your religion and religious beliefs
- Intimidating you with religion ("If you don't do as I say, you'll go to hell.")
- Defiling or destroying books and other materials that represent your philosophical value systems
- Denouncing or rejecting your cultural or ethnic heritage

Physical Abuse

During the relationship you may have experienced physical violence that you may not have labeled as abuse at the time. Not all physical abuse entails broken bones, bleeding, or stitches (these are easily identifiable by anyone as abuse!). Most relationship violence causes damage that others cannot see, so they don't even know it has occurred. Abusers become experts at it. Just think, if your friends, family, and coworkers could *see* the signs of your abuse on a daily or weekly basis, his secret would be out.

Your partner may have pushed or shoved or grabbed you to keep you from leaving the room. He may have twisted your arm sufficiently to cause real pain, but didn't leave a noticeable mark. If he threw you against a wall or pushed you to the floor, no one else would have known. Maybe your abuser strangled you so hard you were gasping for breath, but didn't leave any marks that would allow others to suspect what was really going on. When he did hit you hard enough to leave bruises, he was careful to hit you only on parts of your body that others would not see.

Below is a partial list of examples of physical abuse:

- Pushing
- Shoving
- Hitting
- Grabbing
- Strangling
- Slapping
- Punching
- Biting
- Cutting
- Pinching
- Destroying property
- Hitting with objects
- Hurting or killing pets
- Physically restraining (holding you down, pinning you against a wall, preventing you from moving or leaving, etc.)
- Rape and other sexual coercive acts (see Chapter 4, "The Hidden Horror: Sexual Abuse")
- Physical intimidation (towering over you, blocking your exit, waving his fist, etc.)

A clear understanding of the many forms of relationship abuse and the specific behaviors involved should be helpful in removing al doubt that you were indeed in such a relationship. But beyond these behaviors is the bigger picture of the relationship itself and the process by which the abuse began, continued, and escalated over time.

Why You Stayed

People have probably asked you, "Why didn't you just leave?" Those who have never been in an abusive relationship often find it very difficult to understand how hard it may have been to escape.

You know all too well there were many reasons you didn't get out sooner. Your ex promised to change. You wanted to believe him. You may have thought you just needed to try a bit harder.

Perhaps every time there was an incident of abuse, your abuser told you that it was due to some problem of his: depression, abuse suffered in the past, stress at work. You may have thought that if only you could help get the help he needed for those problems, things would be better.

Perhaps he blamed all the abuse on his drinking or other drug abuse. You repeatedly tried to get him help for his alcohol or other drug problems but nothing ever seemed to work. If it did work, you found that although the abuse may have become more subtle, it remained even after the substance abuse stopped.

Your partner also may have made you worry that if you were to leave, what would you do for money? You may have become dependent upon him for your financial needs. He may have manipulated it so his name alone was on all the bank accounts.

Leaving might have meant that your children would not have both parents in their lives. Your partner may have told you that you would never get custody of the children. You were convinced that you could lose your children if you left, or that your kids needed two parents in their lives.

How many times had he told you that you were useless, stupid, or ugly and that no one else would ever want you? To you, leaving him meant that if he was right, you might be alone for the rest of your life.

And there were the threats. "If you ever leave me..." Your abuser had always followed through on his threats in the past. You believed he would follow through on these threats as well, even if he threatened to kill you.

Or, perhaps it was because of how much you loved him.

How Could You Have Become So Attached to Your Abuser?

You may have asked yourself how it was possible for you to have become so strongly attached to your abuser despite the abuse you suffered. If this was not your first serious relationship, you may feel that, paradoxically, this attachment was somehow stronger and more difficult to break than previous non-abusive relationships. How could this be?

Traumatic Bonding

Traumatic bonding is a theory that tries to explain why abusive relationships create such a powerful connection. Several factors have been identified that must be present for such a bond to form. First, for traumatic bonding to take place a relationship must contain an *imbalance of power*. Power has different meanings to different people, but generally it means that one partner is much more in control of key aspects of the relationship. If your partner made all or most of the decisions, controlled the finances, set himself up as the only "authority," intimidated you through threats or violence, or made you feel powerless in other ways, the power in your relationship was completely lopsided.

The second factor in traumatic bonding is the *sporadic nature of the abusive behavior*. This pattern of on-again, off-again outward abuse and seeming calmness is the strongest form of reinforcement.

The third factor in traumatic bonding involves a kind of *denial*. For emotional self-protection, you told yourself, "It isn't really all that bad." You devised reasons to make the situation seem somehow better than it actually was. You may even have altered your attitudes about the violence itself or found new ways of thinking that disguised the truth from yourself. You may have convinced yourself that your ex-partner had every right to treat you that way because you were late with dinner, forgot to pick up the dry cleaning, or didn't get home exactly on time. You may have thought that if the violence didn't send you to the hospital, it wasn't truly abuse.

Beyond this, even if the abuse was severe, you may have found ways of escaping the violence as it happened by imagining you were outside of your body, looking down on the terrible scene that was occurring. This is another psychological protection strategy called *dissociation*, and it is a powerful tool to create distance between yourself and the violence. Dissociation is discussed further in Chapter 9, "Signs of Unfinished Healing."

These forms of denial and distancing are examples of what psychologists call *cognitive dissonance*. In the case of abusive relationships, cognitive dissonance means that what was happening to you was so horrible, so far removed from your thoughts and expectations about the world, that it was dissonant, "out of tune," with reality. Because you were powerless to change the situation, you relied on internal, emotional strategies to try to make it less dissonant, to make it somehow fit. In other words, to survive, you literally had to change how you perceived reality.

The last factor in traumatic bonding involves *masking the abuse*. Your abuser may not have allowed you to admit the abuse to anyone. Or, you may have escaped the horror of the abuse through the use of alcohol or other drugs. Drinking or using other drugs may have been a way for you to self-medicate. While "medicated," it seemed easier, both mentally and emotionally, to hide from the abuse or violence. It might have also been another way to deny that the problem was abuse and blame the abusive behavior instead on drugs.

These four elements: *unequal power, intermittent abuse, cognitive dissonance*, and *masking techniques*, often combine to create a *traumatic bond* with an abuser. Once this bond is established it becomes terribly difficult to break free of the relationship.

The Stockholm Syndrome

The Stockholm syndrome is another theory about how a person who is being victimized may develop an attachment to an aggressor. This theory grew out of a case in Sweden in 1973 in which bank robbers had held a woman and three others hostage for six days. When they were finally released, the female hostage found she had developed a strong attachment, almost an infatuation, with her captor.

The Stockholm syndrome also assumes four conditions exist that are similar, but not identical to traumatic bonding. One, victims are threatened with death or great physical harm and perceive the perpetrator capable of acting on these threats. Two, victims see no means of escape and, therefore, perceive that their lives depend on the captor. Three, victims feel isolated and hold little hope for outside intervention from family or friends, and, four, the victimizer offers kindness along with the violence, which increases the victims' perception of complete helplessness and dependence on the captor.

This syndrome has, in the decades since the original case, been applied to many victim–victimizer situations. It applies painfully well to abusive relationships where most, if not all, of these conditions often exist. When the syndrome emerges in such relationships, the victim clings to the abuser because that becomes her only hope of survival. This bond, however unhealthy, can sometimes feel stronger even than a bond that grows out of love in a healthy relationship.

Conclusion

An understanding of the behaviors that comprise abuse, as well as a working knowledge of the *often intermittent nature of abuse, traumatic bonding*, and *the Stockholm syndrome*, will help you become more confident that you were in an abusive relationship. It should also help shed light on why you may have struggled so much to leave your abuser and why you stayed in the relationship as long as you did.

Abusive Behaviors Inventory

If you are still wondering if your relationship was abusive, try taking the following quiz. Beside each behavior that applied to your partner, put a checkmark.

Check each of the following that happened on a recurring basis:

_____ Yelled

_____ Called you names

_____ Criticized

_____ Checked up on you

_____ Showed up unexpectedly

_____ Didn't give any emotional support

_____ Always kept track of where you were

_____ Did all the daily planning

_____ Controlled all the finances

_____ Unfairly blamed you

_____ Put you down

_____ Didn't pay attention to you

Check each of the following that happened one or more times:

_____ Threatened

_____ Told you whom you could and could not see

_____ Isolated you from your family

_____ Said he is always "right"

_____ "Towered" over you

_____ Slapped you

_____ Grabbed you

_____ Restrained you

_____ Pushed you

_____ Threatened you with violence

_____ Followed you around

_____ Kicked you

_____ Choked you

_____ Forced sex

If you find that you checked even one of these behaviors, you were likely in an abusive relationship. No two abusive relationships are "equal" and there is no way to compare one to another in terms of level if abusiveness. All are very painful and destructive in their own way. Although some behaviors are clearly more outwardly abusive than others, in general, the more checks, the more abusive the relationship.

This first exercise helped you to identify the abusive behaviors you endured. The next part allows you the opportunity to analyze the effects of these more deeply.

Now, for the following items, explain or analyze briefly how the abusive behaviors affected you.

- List what, if anything, your partner said or did to you to make you feel bad about yourself. Examples of these would be calling you names, telling you that you are stupid or not attractive, or putting you down either to your face or to others. Explain briefly how those behaviors made you feel.

  _____

  _____

  _____

- List the ways, if any, that your ex-partner used to control your relationship. Examples of these would include having the final say in all financial matters, deciding with whom and when you would visit friends or family, what you do, and where you go by yourself or as a couple.

  _____

  _____

  _____

- Explain what effects his control had over your life at the time.

  _____

  _____

  _____

- List what, if anything, your partner said or did that made you think you had no choice but to stay with him. Examples here might be saying that you would never see the kids if you left, no one would believe you about the abuse, or that the abuse would get worse if you ever tried to leave.

———————————————————————————————

———————————————————————————————

———————————————————————————————

- Explain what effects the ability to keep you in the relationship had at the time, such as keeping you from seeing your family, preventing you from going to school, or causing you to lose your job.

———————————————————————————————

———————————————————————————————

———————————————————————————————

- List what, if anything, your partner said or did that made you feel unlovable. Examples include telling you that you were ugly or stupid; you didn't know how to treat a partner; you were a bad lover; and so on.

———————————————————————————————

———————————————————————————————

———————————————————————————————

- Explain what effects his telling you that you were unlovable had over your life at the time. Examples would include isolating you from friends, lowering your self-esteem, or making you believe that you were ugly, stupid, or lazy.

———————————————————————————————

———————————————————————————————

———————————————————————————————

- List what, if anything, your partner said or did to make you feel unsafe or threatened. Examples include increasing levels of violence, promising to find you no matter where you went, making overt threats of injury or death.

  _____

  _____

  _____

- Explain what effects instilling fear in you had over your life at the time. Examples include staying in the relationship, doing everything according to your partner's wishes, or always being afraid of being injured.

  _____

  _____

  _____

These deeper analyses and explanations should help you determine if you were in an abusive relationship. The extent to which the behaviors had a negative impact on you helps confirm that you were in an abusive relationship and opens the door to ending the denial and healing.

2

Are You Out of Danger Now?

Myth: Once you are out of the relationship, you are out of danger.

Myth: There's really no way you can increase your safety.

Myth: If there was no physical violence while you were in your relationship, there won't be any after you leave.

Note: The risk of violence from a former abuser is all too real. You are the person with the most insight to determine to what degree, if any, you are still in danger from your former partner. You know your abuser better than anyone else. However, if you find that others (your therapist, crisis center worker, family, or friends) are telling you that they are more fearful for your safety than you are, be sure to take that into account too. It may be that you are not yet fully ready to acknowledge the true risk that your former partner poses.

If you feel that you are still in danger, the following information is provided to assist you in increasing your safety. The guidelines contained in this chapter should not be interpreted as ensuring complete safety from violence. Remember, *never* let others minimize *your* perception of your risks or make you feel silly about being afraid. Consider the following statistics:

- A victim's risk of getting killed greatly increases when they are in the process of leaving or have just left.
- Nearly three-quarters of the battered women seeking emergency medical services sustained injuries after leaving the batterer.
- Another study found in interviews with men who have killed their wives that either threats of separation by their partner or actual separations were most often the precipitating events that lead to the murder.

These statistics are frightening. But as scary as they are, you know it would have been unthinkable to stay in that relationship rather than to leave it. As you read this chapter and plan for your safety, remember you made the right and smart decision to leave. It took a great deal of courage and inner strength.

What Is Your Risk Level?

Now that you're out, what risks remain? In comparison to living with a violent partner, you may *feel* far safer. However, once you are free of your abusive relationship, concerns about safety may not end; they may escalate. You may still be connected in a variety of ways to your abuser through your children or other family members, or simply because you still live in the same community or go to the same school. However, even if you have broken all these connections, you may still be at risk.

If you experienced a great deal of physical violence in your relationship, ongoing concern for your personal safety makes sense. If your relationship involved controlling behaviors or verbal or emotional abuse, without physical violence, you may think that safety is not an issue for you. Regrettably the level of abuse may increase and become physical after the separation, even if there has been no prior physical violence.

Whether you recently left your abuser or have been out for some time, your former partner may continue to pose a threat to you. Your abuser may not let go of you as you may have thought he would.

If you left, even though your abuser forbade it (which is usually the case), he is probably enraged about no longer being able to control you. The abuse was always about control, and now he may be more desperate than ever to regain that control. His fury now may be beyond what you have witnessed before because he has lost that hold over you and may be desperate to regain it in any way he can.

How can you tell how much risk your abuser poses? It would be great if there were a perfectly reliable predictor of violence after an abusive relationship has ended, but there isn't. The best you can do is look for clues that the likelihood of violence directed at you or your children still exists. Here are some possible indicators that may offer evidence of the continuing danger.

Your Abuser's Behavioral History

Did your ex-partner tell you that if you ever left he would make sure you were never with anyone else? Did your abuser threaten to badly hurt or kill you? Threats of violence and death are obvious and important indicators that you still need to be concerned about your safety. If he followed through on any threats of violence in the past, you have every reason to believe he could follow through on them now that you have left.

Another indicator of increased risk of being hurt or killed by your former partner is his accessibility to weapons. Does he own guns or have access to guns through friends, family members, or work? Does he feel comfortable using a gun? Has your abuser used a gun on you before, in any way? Does your ex have other weapons, such as knives, that were used to threaten you? These factors may indicate an increased risk to you.

Was your abuser increasingly violent toward you? Over the months or years that you were together, did the physical abuse intensify? Did you have the feeling that it was going to continue to escalate if you didn't leave? If so, now that you have separated, his violence may increase even faster.

Think back to references your abuser made about the prospect of your leaving. Were there veiled threats, such as: "You know you really wouldn't want to do that," said in that tone of voice you knew meant violence? Did your abuser directly or indirectly threaten to hurt anyone else that you care about, including your children, family members, or a potential future partner if you left? Did he threaten to destroy your valued belongings or kill your pets if you ever tried to leave? If so, these may be indicators of possible future abuse and violence.

Your Abuser's Psychological History

The majority of people who suffer from psychological disorders are not violent or abusive. However, when determining the threat your abuser poses to you now, you need to consider his psychological history. Is your abuser very impulsive? During your relationship, did he frequently act on a thought or emotion without considering the consequences? People who are impulsive can also be very unpredictable. If this impulsiveness was part of the abuse, the possibility of future violence may be increased.

Did your abuser exhibit rapid or extreme mood changes that led to violence? Was he likely to "fly off the handle" with very little provocation? Was he calm one minute and furious the next? Or perhaps he would seem OK one minute and then suddenly very depressed? Many people who have mood swings are not violent. The danger lies in your former partner's sudden mood swings combined with his need for power and control. If the moods were unpredictable and frightening, you have every reason to believe that this volatility will continue, possibly increasing your risk of future abuse.

Does your ex-partner have a history of depression? Obviously, depression is usually not a sign of violence. However, depression, when combined with a history of controlling and abusive behavior, can increase the risk of future violence. If your abuser is actively suicidal he may feel that what happens to him doesn't matter because he is going to die soon anyway by his own hand. If he feels that he has nothing to lose by hurting or killing you, it will make it easier for him to come after you (this will be discussed in more detail in the next section).

Although people who were abused as children or who witnessed abuse may be more likely to become abusers themselves, this is not an excuse for their abusive or violent behavior. Having endured such abuse may have affected them psychologically, but the choice to act negatively on those emotions is all theirs. Having survived abuse does not give them the right to abuse others, although they will frequently use this as a justification for their actions. If your ex told you he was abused and therefore abused you, remind yourself that he chose to abuse you rather than seeking help to deal with his past, and he may continue to make that choice.

Another area of concern is your former partner's history of alcohol or other drug abuse. If the abuse was more frequent and severe when your partner was doing alcohol or other drugs and he is still actively using, this may increase your risk as well. Alcohol or other drug use does **not** *cause* abuse. However, drug use can give your abuser a convenient excuse for his violence.

Your Abuser's Mind-Set

What does your partner see as the consequences for hurting you now? The less he feels he will lose, potentially the greater the risk to you. If he feels that his life and his freedom (i.e., from prison) are not worth risking violence toward you, the danger might be slightly less.

What your abuser feels he will "lose" by hurting you is a very complicated question. Most likely, many factors influence how he is weighing his potential consequences. If your ex-partner has expressed to you that his life isn't worth living without you, he may feel he has nothing at all to lose by hurting you. If he feels that he could not live with the "shame" (as *he* sees it) of your leaving, this notion might overpower any perceived risk to him.

Did your abuser treat you as property? Did he act as though he owned you? Many abusers objectify their partners and turn them into "things" that are theirs and theirs alone. They do not see their partners as equal human beings. If your abuser treated you this way, he may feel that what "rightfully" belongs to him is gone, and he has every right to do whatever is necessary to get you back or destroy you so no one else can ever have you. Your ex-partner may even try to hurt you physically (such as by scarring or maiming you in some way) so that (in his mind) no one else will want you. If you were merely an object to him, the likelihood of violence toward you now is increased.

What about when your abuser says that he has changed? Perhaps he even tells you that he has been in counseling and is a completely different man. Changing abusive behavior and thought patterns is not easy. If you are considering letting your former abuser back into your life, read Chapter 15, "The Temptation to Go Back," which talks about important issues for you to consider before you take that step.

All these emotional, psychological, and behavioral patterns, when combined with past controlling and abusive behavior, indicate a possible increased risk of violence against you now. The exercise at the end of this chapter will help you assess your current level of risk.

Reducing Your Risk of Violence

Now that you've looked at various factors that may indicate an increased possibility of present or future violence, what can you do to decrease your risk? Unfortunately, there is probably no way to be completely safe. One thing you can do is to take every possible step to reduce your risk. You can begin by assessing your present level of safety.

If you feel an imminent risk that your abuser may find and hurt or kill you, you may need to go into hiding, disappear for a while. If family members or friends live somewhere that your abuser isn't familiar with, you can ask to stay with them temporarily. If this is not an option, you can contact a local crisis center to find out how they can help. Most of these agencies have safe houses where domestic violence survivors can stay safely.

For some survivors, the idea of a "crisis center shelter" conjures up images of housing that is squalid, dirty, and even dangerous. This is not the case. Crisis center shelters accommodate others like you and their children who need a temporary place to stay while they work to help you take back a normal, reasonably safe life.

Making an Escape Plan

If you decide to remain in your current residence, you may want to assess what can be done to increase your safety at home.

If your abuser confronts you, knowing what you are going to do *before* it happens can make a huge difference in your ability to stay safe. In an emergency, seconds count. If your abuser shows up in the middle of the night and starts kicking in your door, you need to have an escape plan in place. If you have made a mental plan of what you would do in this situation, you will most likely react quickly and instinctively to follow it.

What will you do if your abuser enters your home? Think through how you can escape if he comes in by the front door or back door or through a window. If you live in an apartment building, be sure you know the various means of escape such as the elevator, stairs, and all outside exits. You may want to get into the habit of always leaving your essential items in a location that you can access easily and quickly. These include your car keys, some money, your cell phone, a restraining order (if applicable—see the next section), and any medications you and your children take on a regular basis. Make sure you know the fastest route to the local police station. If possible, keep your cell phone with you at all times. Be sure you know how to dial quickly for help in case of an emergency. If you do not have a cell phone and cannot afford one, many crisis centers and police departments have emergency cell phones that they can give you for free.

Another option is to carry a personal alarm system. These alarms are transmitters usually worn around your neck that you have probably seen advertised for the elderly. But they can be lifesavers in a multitude of situations. If you need help in an emergency, you simply push the button on the transmitter and the unit's call center alerts the local police. Some personal emergency systems now come with GPS tracking technology, so the authorities can know exactly where you are.

Once you work out your plan, you may want to avoid sharing it with anyone except others living with you or those you *know* you can trust: who understand your situation, and who might be able to assist you in implementing your plan, such as your therapist, a crisis center worker, or your local police. Think frequently about where you could go at any moment and have a plan ready for how you could escape if your abuser appears. This keeps you one step ahead—and could save your life.

Contact Law Enforcement

You may want to consider informing your local police or sheriff of your situation. You can try to make a personal alliance with at least one officer. Having a law enforcement advocate can help in their better understanding the need to respond immediately in an emergency. You can give the police a full description and a recent photo of your abuser, and any relevant forms, such as copies of restraining orders. Let them know that if you call them, they need to respond immediately. Keep the police department updated. If they are aware of the seriousness of the danger you face, they are more likely to respond quickly and effectively. Also, let the police know of any threats, no matter how veiled, that your former partner has made against you or any family member, friend, or companion. No matter how minor such a threat may seem, it could signal an increase in your risk of violence from him.

You may need to consider obtaining a restraining order against your former partner. This is a legally binding directive that makes it a crime for your ex-partner to threaten, harass, or even approach you and your children. If a restraining order is violated, the perpetrator can be arrested. The exact nature of and procedures for obtaining a restraining order vary by state. Your local police or crisis center can advise you about the exact process. Also, Chapter 12, "Practical Considerations," provides additional information about restraining orders.

Create a Safety Network

In addition to including trusted others in your safety network, it will help if you have easy access to a phone in all parts of your home and that you have a list of important phone numbers right next to them. These numbers can include the police, fire department, and neighbors or close friends on whom you can count to help you and to whose homes you could go. You may want to change to an unlisted phone number and give it only to those who understand your situation. You should also program these numbers into your cell and home phones.

Try to enlist the help of neighbors (you need to have an alternative in case one of the neighbors is not at home). If you feel comfortable with them, you can explain your situation to them, and show them a picture of your abuser. Create a signal or password that indicates they should call the police.

Telling the neighbors or landlord/landlady what you want them to do if they see him enter your house may increase your ability to get help if needed. You can tell them that if they see or hear anything suspicious, they should call the police immediately. You can also share your escape plans with them.

The Children

If you have children who are old enough to understand, include them in your safety plan. Let them know what to do and where to go if your former abuser enters the house against your wishes. You can teach them how to go to a safe place if no trusted adults are at home. Plan ahead for this with your neighbors. You can ensure that once the children are safely in another setting they know to call the police.

If your children are in day care or school or spend time with a babysitter, make sure those adult caretakers know the situation. Being clear about the person or people to whom your children may be released will help ensure their safety. If possible, you can leave photos of your abuser with them so they will know if there is an immediate need to call the police. If your children are named in the restraining order, give copies to their school, day-care center, and babysitters.

Pets

If you have pets, you may want to plan ahead for them as well. Have a leash or pet carrier ready in the event you need to leave quickly. You can look for a place to go to that will take your pets. If you are unable to find such a place, try to find someone else who will care for them temporarily. If you have large animals it may be difficult, but not impossible, to find out where you can take them. Your local crisis center should be able to help you find someone to help you temporarily house your pets.

If you feel you might be in danger, it might be a good idea to install a security system in your home if you can afford one. They are available in a wide range of prices. Some include a panic button that allows you to trigger the alarm from various locations in the house. Another consideration would be to make sure you have good locks on all the accessible windows and doors. Plenty of outside lighting, and, if possible, installing motion-sensing lights could help increase your safety. Try to have some means of escape from all rooms in your house. You may also want to consider locks on the insides of doors to various rooms in the house, particularly on your bedroom door.

Away from Home

Unfortunately, your home is not the only place where you may be at risk. Although your abuser may be more likely to try to confront you at home, you may also be vulnerable to abuse or intimidation at your work or educational setting. Consider making safety plans as you did for your home. You can inform security officers, administrators, receptionists, secretaries, trusted friends, or coworkers of your situation and give them a description or photo of your abuser. As with your plan for home you can plan ahead for how you can leave quickly and be sure you have money and any essentials (such as needed medications) with you. Keeping an extra copy of the restraining order with you at all times ensures that you can easily go to the local law enforcement for help if needed. You might want to make it clear to everyone that they are not to give out any personal information about you to *anyone*. Remember, your ex could enlist the help of another person to call and ask for your address or phone number.

If you have just left a violent relationship or if your ex-partner has recently been making threats, you can always ask that someone escort you to and from your car. Trying to stay in the company of other people at all times, and talking to your supervisor about moving your work station to a more secure, hidden location are other ideas to increase your safety.

If, for any reason, you think your former partner may be stalking you, try never to be by yourself in isolated areas. Be alert. If you ever have the sense you are being followed, you can drive to the nearest police station. If this is not possible, you can go to the nearest highly populated area (a supermarket, mall, restaurant, etc.). It's best not to go home. If your abuser has followed you, you can do something to get people's attention such as blowing the horn repeatedly. Locking your doors, and not getting out of your car are other options. Don't be afraid to call for help. The ability to make an emergency call from the safety of your car can be a lifesaver. (*Note*: Dialing 911 from a cell phone may not work in some areas of the United States. Be sure you know exactly how to make emergency calls from your cell phone.)

Another way to help protect yourself is to learn self-defense. Many police departments, community and women's centers, and colleges and universities offer self-defense classes. These classes help you learn to defend yourself physically and emotionally. They can also help protect you from anyone who might attack you, not just your abuser. In addition, many survivors find that self-defense training helps them to feel greater self-confidence and that they gain an increased sense of control over their lives in general.

If you have been thinking you may need a weapon for protection, be sure to consider this decision very carefully. If you have children in your home, there is always a risk they will accidentally get hurt or killed by the weapon. Obtaining thorough and in-depth training in the use of any weapon will help to ensure you can use it safely. Consult with your local police department to see what they recommend in this regard.

Take Charge

Don't feel embarrassed or ashamed of being assertive to ensure your safety. It's OK not to allow your former abuser to talk you into something you don't really want to do, such as coming into your house or meeting somewhere to talk. If he shows up at your house uninvited, call the police. Some abusers, if arrested, may be less likely to assault their partners in the future.

Don't hesitate to call the police if you ever feel in imminent danger. Some survivors are afraid to embarrass themselves by calling for help if it may not be required. Other survivors convince themselves they are exaggerating the danger and are overreacting. If you are not sure if the situation is going to be dangerous, be willing to err on the side of caution. If you request help that turns out to be unnecessary, this will at the very least alert those you call to the possible danger.

If you live in the home you shared with your abuser, the terms of a restraining order should make the rules and boundaries perfectly clear. If you have a restraining order, your abuser knows that all interaction with you is illegal. There is no such thing as a minor violation of a restraining order. You should report any violation to the police immediately. If you have reason to believe you are in danger and have not obtained a restraining order, you may want to consider filing for one (see Chapter 12, "Practical Considerations").

If or when you move, you may not want to let your abuser know where you live. Think about to whom you give the address and phone number. If you are moving to get away, consider where your ex might logically look for you. If you are moving near a family member or close friend, think about how easily he could find you there. Wherever you go, you may want to get a post office box so your mail is not delivered to your home address.

If Your Abuser Finds You

The key is planning ahead for what you would do if your abuser confronts you. You can think through all the possible scenarios, including home, work, and other public locations. Remember, the number one priority is your safety and that of your children. If the worst happens and you find yourself in a situation where your ex-partner is becoming violent and you cannot escape, do everything possible to incur the least amount of injury. Say whatever you need to say, do whatever you need to do to be safe. This isn't going "backward." This doesn't mean you're weak. This doesn't mean that you are returning to your old ways. It's simply finding a way out of an immediate, dangerous situation and surviving.

If your ex attacks you, make noise. Yelling something like "Fire!" might be more likely to bring help than just screaming. If you are unable to escape or get to an exit, make yourself as small as possible. Get into a corner of a room or under some furniture. Try to cover your head with your arms. Be sure your neighbors understand that they need to call the police immediately if they hear any screams or other sounds of a fight or other trouble or distress.

What All This Means to You Emotionally

Living your life constantly looking over your shoulder can be physically and emotionally exhausting. When a real threat surrounds you every hour of every day, it tends to create unusual behaviors and emotions. You may find that you have a heightened startle reflex. When someone makes a loud noise or touches you innocently from behind, you may jump a mile and your heart may start racing. If you startle easily, especially when entering or exiting a room or other place, this is not a totally unreasonable reaction. It means that you are on your toes, alert to any possible danger. It's a very normal, biological, survival reaction. Your brain and body are working over-time to protect you. As uncomfortable as it may feel, reassure yourself that it is OK to react this way for as long as you are living with this threat.

It is completely normal for you to experience nightmares. The nightmares may be about your abuser finding and attacking you. Or, your nightmares may be more hazy: something bad is happening to you that you can't control. These nightmares may disappear over the coming months or they may hang on for years. Do whatever you need to do to cope with the nightmares. If it helps to sleep with a light on, do it. If you feel more comfortable having friends sleep over, invite them. These are by no means signs of weakness; they are perfectly normal reactions to having survived a terrible ordeal.

Increasing your safety is not easy. While you are taking all the practical steps, don't forget to reward yourself for how far you've come. You decided to leave and you did it. Try to stay optimistic that the day will come when you won't have to worry about being safe. For further discussion of the emotional impact of living under this constant reign of control and violence, see Chapter 8, "When Feelings Overwhelm You."

Finally, if this ever-present threat feels as though it is taking too high an emotional toll on you, perhaps some professional counseling will help you deal with your feelings in healthy and effective ways (see Chapter 13, "Beginning to Heal").

Assessing Your Safety

As stated throughout this chapter, no survivor can ensure complete safety from a former abuser and only you can judge how much safety preparation you may need. This exercise is designed to help you examine ways of increasing and enhancing your level of safety.

Making an Escape Plan

- How will you escape if your abuser comes in through the front door?

  _____

  _____

  _____

- How will you escape if he comes in the back door?

  _____

  _____

  _____

- How will you escape if he comes in through a window? (Write a plan out for each separate room.)

  _____

  _____

  _____

- How will you get out of your apartment building if you can't use your usual exits?

  _____

  _____

  _____

- Where in your apartment or home will you go if your ex-partner gets in and you cannot get out?

_____

_____

_____

Developing a Safety Network

- Do you have access to a phone in all parts of your home? _____

- Do you have a list of important phone numbers next to each phone? _____

- Do you need an unlisted phone number? _____

- Do you have a cell phone? _____

- Are the numbers programmed into your cell phone? _____

- List the names and phone numbers of at least two neighbors who know about your situation and can help you, if needed.

_____

_____

_____

Keeping the Children Safe

- Do you have a code word that alerts them to get out of the house?

_____

- Where will the children go if your abuser breaks into the house?

_____

_____

_____

- What actions should your neighbors take if your children go to their homes?

  _____

  _____

  _____

- Have you explained this plan to the neighbors? _____

- Have you instructed the children's school, day care, and baby-sitters what to do if your abuser shows up there? _____

  _____

  _____

  _____

- Have you provided the children's school, day care, and baby-sitters with a photo of your abuser? _____

Pets

- Do you have a plan for your pets if your abuser breaks in?

  _____

  _____

  _____

Securing Your Home

- Do you have a security system installed in your home? _____

- Do you have secure locks on all outside accessible doors and windows? _____

- Do you have a lock on the inside of your bedroom door? _____

- Do you have motion-sensor lights outside your home? _____

Safety Plan

- Do you have a safety plan in place at work or school? _____

- Have you informed your workplace or school about this plan? _____

- Are you taking alternate routes on your routine trips? _____

Note: It might be a good idea to repeat this exercise periodically in order to ensure you are taking proper precautions on an ongoing basis, and not inadvertently letting your guard down.

3
Self-Esteem

Myth: As soon as the abuse ends, your self-esteem will rebound all on its own.

Myth: Good self-esteem usually comes naturally. It's not something you need to "work" on.

Myth: Abusers just want 100 percent control; they are not targeting your self-esteem.

*T*he power and control your abuser maintained over you were rooted in a number of factors: his belief that he had the right to treat you as his property, the right to treat you in any way he wanted, his decision to abuse you, and his belief that he had control over every aspect of your life. Moreover, one powerful method he most likely also employed was to make you believe that you didn't deserve anything better.

In the beginning of the relationship, your ex might have made you feel that he adored everything about you. You may have felt that in his eyes you could do no wrong. Unfortunately, over time this gradually changed. He most likely slowly started to find fault with little things here and there. He may have begun by saying they were no big deal. As time passed, however, he slowly but surely began to comment on these "faults" more consistently and made it seem as though you were an unworthy person. Your abuser worked relentlessly to chip away at your sense of self-worth. His increasing comments and innuendos caused your self-esteem to take a nose dive. Now, even after you may be out of that abusive relationship, your self-esteem may still be seriously lacking.

Some survivors, particularly if they experienced abuse or neglect in their childhood or in past relationships may have gone into an abusive relationship already having poor self-esteem. If this was the case, your ex most likely picked up on this and knew exactly how to use your lack of confidence against you, what to say and how to act to get right to the heart of your insecurities.

This chapter is designed to help you recognize if, and in what areas, your self-esteem is lacking and to help you improve it. Through this series of exercises, you should be able assess all the wonderful traits you embody: those you already see in yourself and those others see in you. Then you can work on believing in those traits and learning that are you are worthy of love, kindness, and respect.

How Do You See Yourself?

Initially, you will need to find out if you are able to see positive qualities in yourself as much as you see faults. To do this, you will need to take the time to discover who you really think you are now.

Make a List of Your Positive Traits in the Following Categories

Professional Skills

(For example: I'm very hard working and am good at accomplishing tasks, I'm a team player. I'm intelligent)

_____

_____

_____

Interpersonal Skills

(For example: I'm able to have patience and fully attend to friends when they need to talk, I'm a good listener, I'm giving, optimistic, I have a good sense of humor)

_____

_____

_____

Values and Ethics

(For example: I never lie to others, people know they can count on me to tell the truth, I'm honest, I believe in equality for all)

_____

_____

_____

Sense of Physical Self

(For example: I have nice eyes, my hair is a nice color, I keep myself fit)

_____

_____

_____

Outlook on Life

(For example: I am generally optimistic, I am usually upbeat, I have a good sense of humor)

_____

_____

_____

Yourself in Relation to the World

(For example: I am concerned about others' feelings, I am environmentally conscious, I am kind to animals)

_____

_____

_____

Others (Anything You Can Think of About Yourself That is a Positive)

(For example: I care about environment, I like to help others, I'm artistic)

_____

_____

_____

Now go back and see which parts you were unable to come up with anything positive to say or said something negative. Most likely these areas are ones in which your abuser focused on what he said were your "shortcomings."

Often, when coming out of and recovering from an abusive relationship, others may be better than you in seeing the good in you. This exercise is designed to help you see the differences between what you see and what others may see.

Ask friends, family members or even some coworkers who know you fairly well to tell you what positive qualities they see in you. If you want, you can tell them that you are doing some self-esteem work and are asking others for input. Have others either write lists of what they see in you or have them tell you and you can write them down. Every time you get new descriptions from others put those traits into the same categories you used for your own self-assessment.

Professional Skills

(For example: hard working and good at accomplishing tasks, team player, intelligent)

_____

_____

_____

Interpersonal Skills

(For example: able to have patience and fully attend to friends when they need to talk, good listener, giving, optimistic, good sense of humor)

_____

_____

_____

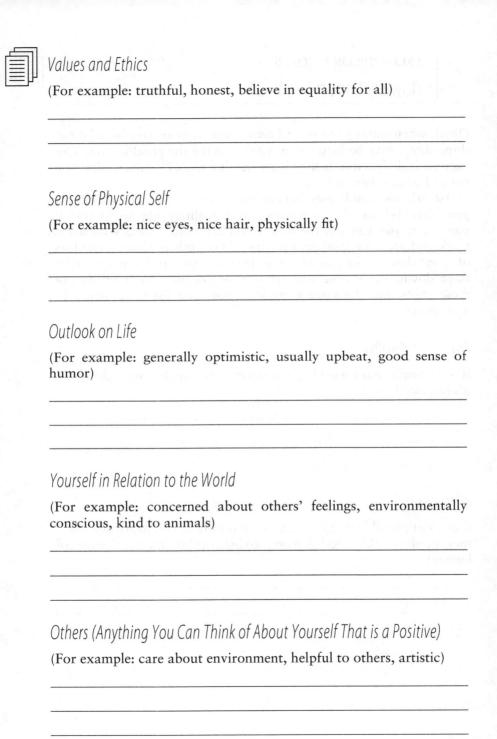

Values and Ethics

(For example: truthful, honest, believe in equality for all)

_____

_____

_____

Sense of Physical Self

(For example: nice eyes, nice hair, physically fit)

_____

_____

_____

Outlook on Life

(For example: generally optimistic, usually upbeat, good sense of humor)

_____

_____

_____

Yourself in Relation to the World

(For example: concerned about others' feelings, environmentally conscious, kind to animals)

_____

_____

_____

Others (Anything You Can Think of About Yourself That is a Positive)

(For example: care about environment, helpful to others, artistic)

_____

_____

_____

Compare the two lists. Were there traits that others pointed out that you do not have on your list? Are there certain areas where what they say about you is completely different? For example do others say that you have beautiful eyes, dress smartly and are graceful, yet you cannot think of a single physical feature of yourself that you like?

If such differences exist those may be the areas you need to work on to develop an overall better view and opinion of yourself.

Are You Too Hard on Yourself?

Reviewing the two lists, do you find that you might be too hard on yourself and tend to make negative comments in your head about yourself (such as: "What an idiot I am! How could I have been so stupid to have forgotten my keys?")? Are there areas where the two lists completely diverged such as others saying what a wonderful friend you are to others while you blame yourself for not doing enough as a friend?

In this *Self-Exploration* you are going to begin by recognizing the ways in which you are too hard on yourself. At first just notice when you are doing it. Don't get mad at yourself or try to stop, just *notice* those thoughts. Spend a week or two getting to know how often and in what ways you are overly critical with yourself.

Next, using the same categories, list some kinder (and probably more accurate) ways of talking to yourself.

Professional Skills

(For example: hard working and good at accomplishing tasks, team player, intelligent)

_____

_____

_____

Interpersonal Skills

(For example: able to have patience and fully attend to friends when they need to talk, good listener, giving, optimistic, good sense of humor)

_____

_____

_____

Values and Ethics

(For example: truthful, honest, believe in equality for all)

_____

_____

_____

Sense of Physical Self

(For example: nice eyes, nice hair, physically fit)

_____

_____

_____

Outlook on Life

(For example: generally optimistic, usually upbeat, good sense of humor)

_____

_____

_____

Yourself in Relation to the World

(For example: concerned about others' feelings, environmentally conscious, kind to animals)

_____

_____

_____

Others (Anything You Can Think of About Yourself That is a Positive)

(For example: care about environment, helpful to others, artistic)

_____

_____

_____

Once you have finished making this list, read it over every day or so. At first it might seem artificial and forced. But try substituting those messages when you notice one of those critical, negative messages arising in your mind. This will seem artificial to you at first but after continual repeating, you will slowly begin to believe that you deserve to be nicer to yourself. Every time you find yourself reverting to one of the negative thoughts, find a way to stop that train of thinking (some people stamp their foot or lightly snap a loose rubber band on their wrist to accomplish this). Substitute in the positive thought. Over time, you will likely begin to believe these positive comments about yourself.

Revisit this list at first daily, then weekly then monthly. See if you can you expand on what you've written to become more inclusive. For example if you wrote "I have nice eyes" see if over time you can say "I have a pretty face." You can revisit and add to this _Self-Exploration_ exercise whenever you want to keep tabs on your progress in this area.

4

The Hidden Horror: Sexual Abuse

Myth: If you are in an intimate relationship, it's not really rape.

Myth: It was sexual assault only if you kicked and screamed and tried to fight him off.

Myth: A rape by an intimate partner isn't as traumatic as stranger rape.

*I*f you were in a controlling and abusive relationship you may also have been subjected to some form of sexual abuse. Many women who are in such relationships have a difficult time accepting that they were, indeed, sexually assaulted by their partner.

It's important to understand that sexual assault is not about sex, but, as with all the abuse in the relationship, it is about *power* and *control*. His sexual desires or drives did not cause him to rape you; it was one more way he could control you. He felt that he had the right to do with you whatever he wanted. He also believed that you had no rights to your feelings or your own body.

Were You Sexually Assaulted?

If your partner touched any private part of your body—your genitals, breasts, or buttocks—against your will, that was sexual assault. Forcing you to dress or act in sexually provocative ways was a form of sexual abuse. Forcing you to do sexual acts that you disliked and were not comfortable with was sexual abuse.

Forcing you to have sex was sexual assault. If penetration occurred, whether it was vaginal, anal, or oral, it was rape. You may have been forced into the act by violence, threats of violence, intimidation, or coercion. Regardless, if you said "no" or indicated you did not want to have sex and he forced you anyway, you were sexually assaulted. Just because you may not have screamed or tried to stop him doesn't diminish the seriousness of what happened to you. A lack of cuts or bruises doesn't imply that it wasn't sexual assault. Because it was your partner or your husband doesn't change the fact that it was sexual assault. No matter what your ex-partner may have said or done, you should *never* have to "submit" to unwanted sex with anyone, including an intimate partner. These acts were one more way your partner could prove he had complete control over you.

In addition to sexual assault, you may have experienced other forms of sexual abuse. If he forced you to be sexual in front of others, that was sexual abuse. If he forced you to be sexual with others that, too, was sexual abuse.

All forms of sexual abuse are degrading and emotionally devastating. Because of numerous myths about sexual assault, some women may not define these acts within the relationship as abuse, but they are.

Sexual Abuse Myths

Many myths about sexual assault and rape persist throughout society. One common belief is that men who rape have unusually strong sexual needs or drives. The truth is, as mentioned earlier, that sexual drive or desire does not cause rape and other sexual abuse. Rapists have not been found to have higher sex drives than non-rapists. Again, sexual assault is rooted in power and control, not sexual drives.

Another myth is that men have a higher sex drive than women, and, therefore, if a man wants sex, his partner must agree regardless of her desire to do so. First this is not always true, but even if your partner wanted sex more often than you did, this does not mean that he had any right to force sex upon you.

An important falsehood to understand about sexual assault is that stranger rape is much more emotionally devastating than rape by someone you know or with whom you are in a relationship. Not only is this not true, but often just the opposite is true. When you are sexually assaulted by someone you know and who claims to love you, the trauma, fear, and horror are overwhelming. The shock may be even more profound than a stranger rape, because this was someone you thought you could trust, someone you chose to be with and whom you thought could never be capable of such an act. Not only did you have to deal with the terror of the sexual assault but you also had to come to terms with the knowledge that someone you thought loved you did this to you. If a stranger had assaulted you, it would usually be easier to say to yourself that he was a maniac or a perverted deviant, rather than someone you once loved and who, you thought, loved you.

How It Happened

Your former abuser may have tried to convince you that it was your duty to satisfy his sexual needs. He may have used religious beliefs (his or yours) to support this idea. You may have believed, and perhaps still do believe, that he had a right to force or coerce sex. Even if you do believe that, it does not reduce the pain and after-effects of the unwanted sexual relations.

If your partner grabbed or touched any private part of your body against your will, you probably felt demeaned and afraid. He may have engaged in his unacceptable touching to demonstrate his ownership of your body. When you aren't able to control what happens to your body, you are rendered powerless. This is exactly how your abuser was trying to make you feel.

Did your abuser use sex as a way to "make up" immediately following an abusive incident? He may have explained that sex was the only way you could prove how much you loved each other. He also may have insisted that sex at that time would prove that everything was OK between you after the violence. You knew that if you refused the abuse might start all over again. After these sexual encounters, you may have felt even more abused and degraded, piling injury upon injury.

Months or years of emotional and verbal abuse often set the stage for sexual abuse. Your abuser may have known that if he "wore you down" long enough, you would become increasingly vulnerable to his sexual attacks. It's more difficult for victims to "fight back" emotionally when they feel bad about themselves, are depressed, scared, or isolated.

Another way your abuser may have forced you into sex was to threaten you with even greater physical violence if you didn't do exactly what he wanted sexually. He always followed through on his threats before, so you had every reason to believe that he would follow through this time. Out of self-protection, you made the choice that refusing his sexual demands was not worth the risk of increasing the physical violence.

He may have threatened to leave you or make life miserable for you if you didn't comply sexually. Enduring the sexual abuse may have been the only way you could escape what you saw as an even worse situation. If this was the case, remember you shouldn't feel guilty. You did what you had to do to survive as best you could. You are not responsible for the sexual abuse. He alone is responsible for that.

You may have suffered the trauma of his forcing you into sexual acts with other people against your will. Not only were you unable to control what was done to your body, you were unable to control who did it. If this happened to you, it might have been even more humiliating and frightening and the fear of what else they might do to you was terrifying. You may have been constantly terrified of the possibility of getting pregnant or contracting HIV or other sexually transmitted diseases.

Your former partner may have forced you to have sex with others for money. He may have profited from your abasement and fear. If you were forced to do this, it is important to realize that in many ways you were being kept as a slave. You felt you had no way to escape these horrors. Again, you endured these humiliations to survive.

All of these forms of sexual assault and exploitation may make you feel embarrassed and ashamed even though *you did nothing wrong*. Your abuser made you do things you otherwise would never have done. They in no way reflect your true desires or who you really are.

The Effects of Sexual Abuse

The effects of sexual abuse can be numerous and sometimes long lasting. Understanding how the abuse may have affected you can start you on the road to healing.

PTSD

PTSD or *post-traumatic stress disorder* is a term for the effects some people experience after they have survived trauma. We are most familiar with PTSD in connection to those individuals who have been in war, on the battlefield. We talk about the various psychological issues they experience months and sometimes years later such as nightmares, residual fear, and spontaneous flashbacks to the traumatic experience. What we know now is that PTSD can occur as a result of a wide range of traumas including those experienced in abusive relationships. This chapter discusses many of these effects that someone who has lived through abuse may experience after they are out of the relationship, sometimes for years.

Shock

If you are like many women, you may have experienced a state of shock after the sexual assaults. Even if you had endured other forms of abuse from your former partner, the sexual assault may have seemed like something that would never happen. Many women say that during the actual sexual abuse episode and for weeks, months and sadly at times years after, they felt as though in a dream, a nightmare from which they couldn't awaken. What happened was so out of context with everything they believed about life and relationships, it didn't fit into reality.

You probably suffered from nightmares. The nightmares may have been reenactments of the assault or they may have depicted other terrifying occurrences that you were unable to escape. Your nightmares may have been exaggerated by having to sleep in the same bed with the person who did this to you.

Denial

After the sexual assault, you may have tried to block the entire event from your conscious mind. You may have avoided thinking about it at all for quite some time. On the other hand, you may have remembered it, but your memory somehow altered it to be much less traumatic than it actually was. Only later, when you were out of the relationship and safe, did something trigger your memory of the event and the full impact of what happened finally hit you. Perhaps days, weeks, or months later, the assaults may suddenly have overwhelmed you.

If you did manage to push the horror aside for a while, it is very important you recognize why the denial happened. Unfortunately, many women blame themselves for not realizing sooner just how bad the sexual assault was. They worry that if they had realized it sooner, they could have left sooner. Usually, this is not the case. If you managed to suppress the trauma of what was happening, it was for a good reason. Feeling the full psychological force of the sexual abuse at the time it happened might have made you unable to go on. It could have made you feel trapped and see your life as totally unbearable. You might have become deeply depressed and possibly suicidal. Denial probably helped to save you.

Isolation

The sexual assaults may have caused you to become even more isolated than you were already. The guilt, embarrassment, depression, and decreased self-esteem may have made you avoid the very people who might have been able to help. Trying to talk about or explain this part of the abuse may have been just too much for you.

Self-Esteem

Other reactions in the days following the abuse may have been the feeling of being dirty and ashamed. You might have taken numerous showers or baths and still not felt clean. If you felt comfortable with your body before the assault, that might have changed. You may have begun to feel ashamed of your body and wanted to hide any hint of sexuality by wearing baggy clothes, neglecting your personal hygiene, and even changing your eating patterns.

If, like most victims of abuse, you saw no way out of the relationship, then you may have stayed with your partner for some time after the sexual abuse began. As with all the forms of abuse, the sexual abuse probably came and went. At times, your partner may have seemed very caring, understanding, and even sensual rather than intimidating and frightening. If you resumed sexual relations with him, this is one more piece of evidence that points out how complicated and perplexing these relationships can be. It does not mean you are a bad person for having sex with him voluntarily.

Trust

If your partner sexually assaulted you, you know firsthand the confusion and the complex mix of emotions you experienced. If your trust in your partner had not already been completely destroyed, it certainly was now. If you stayed in the relationship, you probably began to question what else he might do to you. If he could do something this hateful, were there no limits to his abuse?

Perhaps you started to question your ability to judge who is trustworthy and who is not. After all, you originally trusted this man and believed that he would never hurt you. In reality, you had no way of knowing that he was capable of doing such a thing, yet you may have spent a great deal of time beating yourself up for not seeing this coming. Just as with the other forms of abuse you endured from him, a sexual assault was probably unimaginable before it happened.

Fear

Even though the person who sexually assaulted you was your intimate partner, you may have feared that if he was capable of rape, he might be able to kill you. Even if there was no other violence before this, you still may have feared for your life. Sexual assault was so unthinkable, you probably couldn't even guess what he might do to you next.

If you had already experienced physical violence from your abuser, the fear of violence at the time of the sexual assault may have been greatly heightened. And after the sexual violence you probably felt that the threat of all kinds of violence from your partner was much greater.

Now, after escaping the abusive relationship, you may still have a heightened sense of fear, particularly of people touching you or of any attempts to become physically intimate with anyone else.

Anxiety and Hypervigilance

After you were assaulted, you may have found your overall level of anxiety was greatly increased. Everyday events unrelated to the sexual attacks created high levels of worry and concern. You may have developed headaches, backaches, or stomachaches. Your neck may have felt stiff and painful. You also may have become more "jumpy" following the sexual assault. If there was a sudden loud noise, you may have felt you jumped a mile. If someone, without your knowledge, touched you from behind, you were extremely startled. You flinched, your heart raced, and you broke into a cold sweat. You may have felt as though you were always on alert, ready for something bad to happen. This reaction, known as *hypervigilance*, may have lasted for weeks, months, or years.

You also may have experienced a psychological condition called *intrusive recall*; this means that suddenly, without warning, your mind becomes immersed in thoughts of the assault. This recall would, at times, happen out of the blue. It may have felt like a horrible daydream or it may have seemed more like a flashback. It was almost as if the assault was happening all over again. You may have reacted verbally or physically to such a flashback by yelling, crying, or curling up into a fetal position. Any of these reactions to trauma, hypervigilance, and intrusive recall, are discussed further in Chapter 9, "Signs of Unfinished Healing."

Sexual Feelings

The sexual abuse you endured may have ended any sexual desire you had for your abuser. After the first episode, you may have wanted never to be sexual with him again. This is a very normal reaction to such a horrible event. From then on, all sexual contact with him may have felt like another sexual assault.

As with the other forms of abuse, he may have convinced you that he was sorry and that it would never happen again. You wanted to believe him, and although the assault did great damage, you may not have "blamed" your partner at first. You tried to get past it and you may have even returned to a consensual and desirous sexual life with him.

If during any part of the sexual abuse your body became sexually aroused, he may have tried to convince you that, therefore, you really wanted and liked it. Nothing could be further from the truth. Remember, physical responses to direct stimulation are sometimes possible regardless of your emotional and psychological reactions. Regardless of any arousal you may have experienced during the abuse, no one likes or wants to be sexually abused.

Depression

Perhaps the most common reaction to sexual assault is depression. You probably reached the point when you felt an overwhelming sense of sadness and loss. He took something precious away from you: control over your body, your feelings, and your life. In a matter of minutes or hours, he took a huge part of you that it may take you a long time to regain. This depression was caused not only by the realization of all you lost, but also by the knowledge that someone you had trusted and loved had violated you. If you were already depressed, this assault may have made it much worse.

While depressed, your eating and sleeping patterns may have changed. Suddenly, you may have had difficulty falling or staying asleep. In every waking moment, you were so emotionally distraught by the sexual assault that it wasn't possible to sleep much at all. On the other hand, you may have slept all the time, trying to escape any thought or memory of what had happened to you. Your depression may have caused similar changes in your eating patterns. Eating concerns will be discussed more in the "Self-Destructive Behaviors" section later in this chapter.

Your depression may have been accompanied by fatigue. Everyday activities may have seemed overwhelming. Simple tasks like brushing your teeth or making a meal may have seemed insurmountable. You may have found yourself losing interest in activities you used to enjoy, such as working out, enjoying music, reading, or crafts.

As discussed earlier, your self-esteem may have been influenced by this sexual attack as much or more than by the other types of abuse you may have suffered. If you felt OK about yourself prior to the sexual abuse, you may have found you hated yourself afterwards. This loss of self-esteem probably stemmed not only from the depression, but also from self-blame and anger. If your belief in yourself was shaky to begin with, the assault may have destroyed it completely.

One of your partner's primary goals was to ensure that you would stay with him. The sexual attack may have convinced you that you were unworthy of anyone else's love. Consequently, if you thought you didn't deserve to be treated better, you may have found even greater difficulty in attempting to leave the relationship. The sexual assault was one more way for him to keep you right where he wanted you.

If your depression became too intense, you may have become suicidal. Sexual assault combined with feeling trapped in the relationship may have made you decide life was not worth living: but you didn't kill yourself. That you are still here is an incredible testament to your inner strength.

Anger

Another normal reaction to sexual assault is anger. Some women feel an overpowering rage that consumes every thought and feeling. But in your situation if you dared to display your anger, the situation would have become much worse. Instead of being able to vent your anger, you had to repress it, bottle it up inside of yourself.

You may have taken your anger out on those around you other than your abuser: your children, family, friends, or coworkers. This may have been the only way in which you could release some of that fury. Or you may have taken the anger out on yourself. Maybe you started to blame yourself for getting into this horrible situation in the first place. You may have even started to hate yourself. This self-hate may have caused you to seek other ways to hurt yourself.

Self-Destructive Behaviors

Increasing your alcohol or drug use may have been a way for you to deal with the anger and cope with the pain. These drugs may have been a way for you to self-medicate, to try to stay "sane."

If the attacks made you want to bury your sexuality, you may have thought that by altering your body, you would become less sexually desirable. You thought that if you were less attractive, maybe the assaults would end.

Perhaps you found yourself eating much more than you had before in order to gain weight. In your mind you may have thought that being overweight would make you less sensual. Or you may have tried to do just the opposite. You may have reduced your eating and lost a lot of weight. You may have felt that by becoming very thin you would become less sexual, your chest would be flatter, you would have a more boy-like figure. You may have also perceived a bit of control over at least one part of your life: your eating.

Self-injurious behaviors such as cutting yourself may have been another outlet for your anger and distress. If, after being raped, you felt nothing or felt anger toward yourself, cutting may have become a routine. If you cut yourself, perhaps it was to feel something at a time when you seemed completely numb. Cutting yourself may also have been an attempt to punish yourself for what you thought was somehow your fault.

What Now?

Now that you are out of the abusive relationship, one of the things that you may find very difficult is coming to terms with your sexuality. If you were sexually assaulted, you may find that you now feel no sexual desire at all, for anyone. This is a common reaction after such abuse. The healing process can take a long time and involves not only healing your feelings of self-esteem and sexual desire but also healing your ability to trust another person.

On the other hand, you may have started having sexual interactions with a number of different people. This may have been a way for you to feel back in control of your own body. It may have been your way to avoid an emotionally intimate relationship with someone. Or you may have been searching to regain your prior enjoyment of your sex life.

Any one or a combination of these reactions to sexual assault may have felt devastating. Trying to cope with the reality of it at the same time you were experiencing nightmares, jumping at every noise or touch, and reliving the incident in your mind over and over again, may have made you feel as if you were truly going crazy. You were, of course, having a *normal* reaction to a horrible and terrifying trauma.

Everyone is different and each abused person suffers varying after-effects from sexual abuse. There is no timetable for when you "should" be over these symptoms. Some effects come on quickly and last for weeks or months. Others may not begin until much later and last for a very long time.

If you were sexually assaulted, you might experience events throughout your life that may trigger old reactions of fear, depression, anxiety, anger, or mistrust. Over time, these reactions should become more bearable, but they might never go away completely.

You may not always know exactly what triggers these responses. It may be obvious events such as a movie in which a rape occurs, or it might be as subtle as passing someone in the street who is wearing the same cologne your abuser wore.

If you find yourself having such a reaction, even if you don't know why, it's OK. There is no mental-health milestone you have to pass at any certain time. You are *not* crazy for having these reactions whether it's been a month, a year, or five years, or more. They are perfectly normal.

However, you will not always feel as bad as you do right now. Survivors of rape and other forms of sexual abuse talk about the pain slowly lifting. If the pain you feel is particularly acute or if you find that the pain is not getting better as time goes by, then you may want to get extra professional help and support.

You may find it helpful to find a survivor's support group, either in person or online. Talking with other victims who went through a similar experience can be very empowering. You may also want to talk with someone from a local crisis center or a therapist who specializes in this area (see Chapter 13, "Beginning to Heal"). Getting help does not mean you are weak. It means you are taking care of yourself.

Remember, the sexual assault or assaults were not your fault. You did nothing to bring them on, and you in no way deserved to be treated like that. Over time your reactions and feelings stemming from the attacks should fade as you regain the life you want. Also, as time goes on, you will be able to recognize with clarity and confidence that you do not deserve to be hurt ever again; not by anyone, including yourself.

Self-Talk

It is often so difficult to talk to anyone about sexual abuse that people keep their feelings bottled up inside. Now that you are out of the abusive relationship, it may be time to start exploring what you went through and why it may still be affecting your self-esteem and sexual life. This exercise involves remembering and examining what you went through, what it took to survive, and how the abusive relationship may be affecting you now. Completing this exercise may bring up some uncomfortable feelings stemming from the abuse, but being able to face those feelings is part of healing and moving on with your life.

The worst thing my partner did to me sexually was _____

_____

_____

_____

The part that comes back into my mind most often is _____

_____

_____

_____

The most difficult part of remembering what he did to me is _____

_____

_____

_____

I made it through the sexual abuse by _____

_____

_____

_____

When I think about getting into another sexual relationship I *feel*

_____

_____

_____

When I think about getting into another sexual relationship, I think

_____

_____

_____

Since escaping the relationship, the ways in which my sexual life has

changed are _____

_____

_____

_____

We suggest that you complete this *Self-Exploration* exercise again in a month or two to help you track your progress. You will hopefully notice that your discomfort in thinking about these issues and the negative effects of them on your present life have diminished. If, instead, you find that your emotional reactions continue to run high and still interfere with your ability to cope with your life, that may be a sign that your healing process is stalled and perhaps some counseling would be a good idea.

5

How Could You Have Loved an Abuser?

Myth: Once someone has abused you, all your love for him vanishes.

Myth: Anyone who could love an abusive partner must have a serious psychological problem.

What Is Love?

Life would be so much easier if love were always rational and predictable: You find the right person, you fall in love, you treat each other with respect, tenderness, and caring, and you live happily ever after. Unfortunately, love is not rational. Love does not always live up to expectations. Love isn't even always based on how you are treated. Love is a very rich, complex, and often puzzling set of emotions and behaviors. People often fall in love without really knowing everything about their partner, without knowing for sure how they will be treated. And once in love, people find that "falling out of love" can be very difficult.

When this is true in an abusive relationship, it can be extremely confusing. Some survivors feel hatred or nothing at all toward their abusers, but many others torture themselves with painful questions: "How could I have loved him after what he did to me?" "My ex hurt me, was cruel to me, so how could I still have those feelings for him?" "Doesn't this mean there is something wrong with *me*?" The answer to this last question is: "No!" These feelings and questions are common and perfectly normal among survivors.

It Was So Good at First

You probably recognized your relationship was controlling, abusive or violent. You may have known it was fundamentally unhealthy. But abusive relationships do not start out that way. On the contrary, things were wonderful at first. Your ex was attentive, caring, charming, and committed. You felt attraction for many reasons. When you think back to the early days of the relationship, you can picture all the gifts, how he wanted to be with you all the time, and how he told you he loved you more than anyone else ever could.

No one, not even your abuser, is all good or all bad. Most abusers have some genuinely good characteristics: the ones that made you fall in love. Characteristics such as being so charming, a good sense of humor, attentiveness to your needs, an interesting skill or hobby, a passion for reading, or a special physical attractiveness may be attributes that drew you into the relationship. Unfortunately, as time went on, you realized that all these positive qualities could not override the control and abuse.

Early in the relationship, your abuser may have awakened in you brand-new emotions about yourself; maybe for the first time you felt you deserved to be treated well. You felt lucky to have found such a loving, devoted partner. At the beginning, you may have felt he treated you better than anyone ever had before. At the beginning your ex-partner was probably protective, generous in some ways, very complimentary toward you, and even jealous. You may have seen that jealousy as a flattering sign of how much he loved and cared for you. Thinking back, you can remember conversations between the two of you about special and rare qualities of your relationship.

If you came into this relationship with a history of childhood abuse or abuse in other intimate relationships, you may have had greater difficulty in immediately recognizing the danger signs. Some survivors who have endured repeated abuse may fail to realize that they deserve or should expect anything better (see Chapter 17, "Loving Again"). This by no means excuses the abuse or makes you somehow to blame. It simply may help you to let go of some of your guilt or confusion about not acknowledging the abuse earlier.

Recognizing the Signs of Abuse

It is very painful to discover now that many of your former partner's "special" characteristics were actually signs of the abuse to come. The attentiveness, possessiveness, and jealousy that seemed so charming and endearing turned into control, abuse, and violence. With this discovery may come the feeling that you failed in some way. And you didn't see it coming. In the aftermath of the relationship you may have begun to question your own ability to find a healthy relationship.

Giving up that relationship may have felt as though you were also abandoning your ability to love and be loved. It can take time after leaving an abusive relationship to understand that some of your former partner's qualities, which initially attracted you were, in fact, not healthy ones. However, this does not mean that you are not capable of loving someone truly and deeply. It also does not imply that you are unworthy of being loved in return in the same way.

Why Couldn't You See the Changes?

Another difficulty survivors often face is identifying when the relationship went from good to bad. When did it change? Why wasn't there a specific point when you said, "That's it. I will no longer love this person"? If this question feels difficult or even impossible to answer, that's because it is. Usually, abuse creeps into a relationship in an insidious, gradual way, over months or years. A precise moment or single event that defines the beginning of the abuse rarely exists. Several points may help you to understand this.

Think about what else was happening in your relationship as the abuse was growing. Chances are your love, caring, and devotion for him were growing as well. The love came first and then kept pace with the abuse. To try to pinpoint the moment when the abuse outweighed the love you felt may not be possible even now.

Identifying the beginning of the abuse is made more confusing by the fact that abusive relationships are not overtly abusive all the time. Some of the time the controlling behaviors were so well hidden they were barely recognizable. The outward "signs" of abuse and violence may have been intermittent, described in Chapter 1, "Were You in an Abusive Relationship?"

Many factors may have helped to keep the relationship going and kept your feelings of love alive after the abuse began. Your partner likely made promises to you: "I promise this will never happen again," "I promise I'll change." You believed these promises the first time. And most likely the second. And more. As the abuse continued, the claims of remorse may have increased; the promises to change may have become more persistent. You continued to believe him. You wanted to believe him. After all, you were in love.

Then there were all the apologies. Your abuser seemed truly sorry. You offered forgiveness. Now, however, when you think back, you realize the apologies were conditional. They blamed you! "I'm sorry, but if only you hadn't..." They always made the abuse somehow your fault. You may have begun to believe this, and you may even remember apologizing for your actions. You began to believe that if you were careful about what you said or did, you could prevent the abuse from happening again. As the abuse escalated over time, the blaming became more obvious. "I didn't mean to hurt you, but if you just weren't so (stupid, ugly, careless, dumb, etc.), this would never have happened." Time after time you were made to believe that every act of violence or abuse was your fault. Day after day you were made to feel that you were unworthy.

To convince you further that you were at fault, he probably told you that the abusive behavior had never happened in any other past relationship (this was almost surely not true). You may have even known a past partner, but never heard a word about abuse or violence. Therefore, you were inclined to believe that it must be something about you, something wrong with your ability to love. Now, looking back, you realize that you never said a word to anyone either.

"If you really loved me..." Did you hear this a lot? Throughout your time together this and other similar statements were calculated to let you know that if you only had the capacity to love him enough, or somehow "better," the relationship would work. Your partner explained that the abusive acts were the result of your inability to love him enough. Eventually, you may have begun to believe this. But, the truth is that your love wasn't inadequate or wrong—it was your partner who was unable to love anyone without power and control.

Why Did You Stay?

In hindsight, looking back at the relationship you may have asked yourself, "Why didn't I leave sooner?" One reason may have been that as your abuser was making you feel unworthy of him, he was also working to make you feel you were unworthy of everyone else too, that it would be impossible for you to find anyone else to love you, ever. So, you thought if you stayed and tried to behave in ways that would please him, you could avoid the abuse and would at least not be alone.

Perhaps you tried to discuss with others your growing doubts about your relationship. If so, you may not have received much support. Most abusers are very skilled at keeping that part of themselves hidden from the outside world. Others see them as charming, likable people. Those you confided in may have implied that you should try harder to make the relationship work. They were not willing to blame your partner, so again you thought it must be you who was "unlovable."

At those times your partner admitted to treating you poorly (if he ever made such an admission), he placed the blame on his past, on being abused as a child. Your partner may even have asked for your help in recovering from his trauma. Again, the responsibility was placed on you to heal him. Also, your partner may have blamed his abuse on other outside factors such as a bad day at work, stress over finances, or someone else who made him angry. You may have felt sorry for him and believed that if you didn't try to help, you must not really love him. This became another justification for loving him. Your partner seemingly needed you, and you thought that once you helped him heal, he would stop abusing you.

Another complicating factor in understanding your abusive relationship is that certain cultural norms or religious teachings reinforce the notion that women should love their partners, no matter what.

In some cultures, it is the woman who is held responsible for the success or failure of a relationship. In others, abuse is seen as something a woman must endure. Your partner may have used these beliefs against you, citing religious writings or other materials to justify his violent behavior (see Chapter 1, "Were You in an Abusive Relationship?"). If you were raised with such beliefs, they can interfere with your ability to recognize that the abuse was wrong. Your beliefs may have made it more difficult to stop loving him and may even have strengthened your resolve to stay with him and continue loving him.

You probably spent a long time loving your abuser before you finally realized just how bad the situation was. Then you probably spent more time hoping and believing things would change. Next you believed it was all your fault. It's unrealistic to think that these feelings would have disappeared overnight. All the justifications, rationalizations, and excuses you used and believed for so long became part of your perception of yourself and of him.

Every time you wonder how you could have loved such a person, stop to consider what it says about you as a loving person. If you didn't love your ex-partner so much, this would not be so difficult. Despite what he told you during that relationship, this shows how deeply you can care for another. It is time for you to become strong, to love yourself as much as you can love a partner. Now that you are free of the abuse, you can begin to re-create the love for yourself that he stole from you. This, in turn, will help you become a person who will demand to be treated by your next partner with as much love and respect as you will offer in return (see Chapter 17, "Loving Again").

SELF-EXPLORATION
Why You Loved Your Abuser

You are probably aware that your ex-partner possessed some positive traits. If you are condemning yourself about your past or present feelings, it can be helpful for you to remember why you fell in love with him. This *Self-Exploration* exercise is designed to offer you that opportunity.

List the characteristics that originally attracted you to your ex-partner (such as certain personality traits, hobbies, profession, physical appearance, etc.).

1. _____

2. _____

3. _____

4. _____

5. _____

6. _____

7. _____

8. _____

9. _____

10. _____

Other: _____

Now, compare this list with your answers to the *Self-Exploration* exercises in Chapter 1: "Abusive Behaviors Inventory" and "Abusive Behaviors Analysis." This comparison should help you to understand better how you could have loved an abusive partner and why you needed to end it.

6

Abuse of Men by Women, and Abuse in Gay, Lesbian, and Transgender Relationships

Myth: Only women can be victims of abuse.

Myth: A man can stand up for himself against any abuser.

Myth: Abuse does not exist in gay and lesbian relationships.

Survivors of relationship abuse have endured many painful and traumatic events and most must continue to deal with the effects of these traumas after freeing themselves of their unhealthy relationships. Some do not fit into the typical "mold" of abusive relationships: heterosexual relationships in which the male is the abuser. In other types of abusive or violent relationships, the suffering the victim faces is equally traumatic, and some issues they face and are trying to cope with now may be unique and even more difficult.

Men as Victims of Abuse by Women

As noted in the introduction, the majority of victims of abuse are women and the abusers are men. Obviously, however, this is not always the case. Because of social stereotypes that label men as able to take care of themselves, especially physically, men who are survivors of abuse have unique difficulties in recognizing, surviving, and escaping an abusive relationship. The embarrassment, shame, and fear may be even more exaggerated. Cultural myths about the roles of men and women in our society, layered on top of the usual reasons victims fail to find help, may cause survivors to meet with unique obstacles, both while they endure the relationship and after they escape from it.

If you are a man who was in an abusive heterosexual relationship, you probably first went through a stage of disbelief when the abuse began, followed by the hope that you could change her. These feelings may have been reinforced by society's myths that all women are nurturers, they are supportive and caring, they are passive and non-aggressive. These stereotypes about women were probably coupled with those about men: not nurturing, unemotional, in control, assertive, aggressive. Even as the abuse began and increased, these cultural expectations may have delayed your ability to recognize that you were indeed in an abusive relationship.

As time went on and you finally began to recognize the problems, you may have tried reaching out to others. Unfortunately, the friends and family you talked with may have downplayed the seriousness of what was happening, may have laughed at you with derisive comments such as, "How on earth could a woman scare you?" Or they may have completely dismissed what you said as your problem for not being enough of a man. All these unsupportive attitudes may have caused you to believe the problems were really all your fault, or at a minimum, prevented you from any further attempts to reach out to others for help, advice, or consolation. It should be noted that most men would not be violent with a woman.

It is easier for women who are abusers to mask their abusive behaviors from the outside world. The culture starts from the position that women could never be abusers, and such women can use that to their benefit, especially in public settings. Your abuser probably could get away with many insults, put-downs, and controlling behaviors because, although others may see these as negative qualities, they rarely will label them in their own minds as part of an *abusive* relationship.

Verbal and emotional abuse are less likely to be recognized as abuse within any relationship. Within a heterosexual relationship in which the victim is the man, he is assumed by the culture to be the one in control. Consequently, many outsiders may have said to you something along the lines of, "If you don't like it just tell her to stop!" You may have even heard the old adage "Who wears the pants in your family?" This dig is obviously directed at you not your abuser. The idea that the victim is responsible for the abuse is once again reinforced.

Your abuser may use these common myths to increase your sense of insecurity and responsibility for the abuse. She may have told you that you aren't really much of a man, that you are supposed to be taking care of her and you are doing a lousy job at that, or that you are a failure as a provider. As in any abusive relationship, such attacks chipped away at your self-esteem and personal confidence. Once free of these accusations, the effects of them typically do not fade quickly. For many male survivors of female abuse, professional support and counseling may be necessary to focus on and work through these potentially debilitating issues. The staff at most domestic violence crisis centers are trained and experienced in assisting male survivors. Usually, if a shelter does not accommodate men, the staff will make other arrangements in the community for a safe house if a male survivor needs to escape.

Abuse within Same-Sex and Transgender Relationships

Unfortunately, domestic violence and relationship abuse are believed to be equally common in same-sex couples. The rate of abuse in transgender relationships is not well known but most likely equals that of other relationships. Estimates of the prevalence of abuse in same-sex relationships range from 20 percent to 33 percent, which is about the same as in heterosexual relationships. Again, although the majority of this book deals with female survivors of abusive opposite-sex relationships, much, if not most, of the material applies to all intimate abuse. However, among same-sex and transgender couples, some additional concerns should be discussed.

Society's Expectations

The cycle of violence and wide range of emotions that rolled over you time and time again probably was exacerbated by the layers of negative beliefs, rejection, and irrational fears some people hold toward gay, lesbian, and transgender individuals and couples (homophobia). When a society views the world as innately heterosexual, that heterosexuality is the norm, and that anyone in an intimate relationship is assumed to be with someone of the opposite sex, that's heterosexism. Homophobic and heterosexist attitudes usually imply that same-sex couples are bad, wrong, immoral, but even worse, they often simply deny you and your partner's existence: You become invisible.

It is difficult enough for *heterosexual* individuals to talk about their abuse, but when you include the fact that much of the world doesn't understand or even acknowledge the existence of relationships that are other than heterosexual, you can see why you may have experienced a much more difficult task in finding support and assistance during and after your abusive relationship. When you tried to talk to heterosexual family members or friends, they may have discounted your pain and your relationship, because to their way of thinking you could just leave and go find another "friend." They may discount the depth of feeling in gay and lesbian relationships and lack the ability to empathize at all. You may have walked away from those conversations feeling even more isolated and "different" than ever before.

Myths

As mentioned in Chapter 3, many myths about the roles of men and women exist in most societies. For example, if women are "always supportive, caring, and passive," how is it possible that they are ever the abusers in an intimate relationship? But they can be the abusers in both heterosexual and lesbian relationships. Or, on the other hand, if men are "always in control, non-emotional, and aggressive," how could they possibly be abused? But they can be abused in both heterosexual and gay relationships. The myths that affect partners in heterosexual relationships also affect people in same-sex and transgender relationships, often to an even greater extent.

Perhaps the most common falsehood about gay, lesbian, or transgender relationships is that the individual has made a conscious *choice* about their sexual orientation or gender identity. If others believe you *chose* to be in a same-sex relationship or somehow *chose* your transgender identity, they are likely to be less sympathetic both to your choice and to the fact that your relationship is abusive. In fact, they may blame you. These identities are *not* choices, they are part of who someone is as a human being.

Another of society's most common false beliefs is that the love between same-sex couples is different, that it cannot possibly be as strong or as committed as the love between a man and a woman. In other words, too many people understand love to refer only to *heterosexual love*. This belief causes some heterosexual people to minimize your love, and, as a result, minimize the abuse. This, then, further increases the chance that many in the heterosexual community will dismiss your emotional pain, will not understand what is happening to you, and you will be left feeling even more isolated than you were before you spoke to them. Finding a counselor you trust or a support group of others in similar situations can provide great support and comfort during your healing process by helping you realize you are not alone.

Another common myth relating to gay male couples in particular is that sadomasochism (S&M) is particularly common in such relationships. Although this belief is untrue (such activities are equally prevalent for couples of all sexual orientations), such a misconception causes many survivors to fear that abuse will be dismissed as just a "normal" part of "that kind of a relationship."

One final myth that may have influenced your ability to reach out was the belief that male-on-male violence is more common than woman-on-woman violence. This is untrue. If you were in an abusive lesbian relationship, this myth may have increased your fear that no one would believe you.

Lack of a Support Network

During your abusive relationship you may have tried to reach out to support systems such as counselors or advocates, but even they may have made you feel alone, too, especially if they were not trained specifically in abusive relationships. If you tried to talk to them, they may have immediately assumed you were in a heterosexual relationship, making comments about "your opposite-sex partner." They may have failed to acknowledge, as so many others do, that perhaps your partner was the same sex as you. If you explained that your partner was the same sex, they may have reacted with surprise, discomfort, or inappropriate questions and curiosity. All of these things may have forced you back into silence. These kinds of reactions also support the false notion that the abuse is somehow your fault. As a result you may have become less likely in the future to attempt to find help due to fear of discrimination, embarrassment, or further blame (see "Resources" at the end of the book for organizations where you can find help).

Another difficulty that victims and survivors in same-sex or transgender relationships encounter involves a tactic abusers use to protect themselves: the abuser pretends to be the victim. In opposite-sex couples when the abuser is male, the roles of abuser and victim are usually clear and identified more easily by others. For same-sex or transgender couples, however, this may not be so obvious. Therefore, in an effort to conceal his or her abusive behavior, an abuser may access the same outside support agencies that are needed by the victim. Once this happens, counselors or crisis centers usually provide support for only one partner, and cannot serve both. The burden to "prove" who is truly the abuser falls to the victim and may be feel more difficult than it is for women in heterosexual relationships. Crisis center staff should, however, be trained in identifying what is called the "predominant aggressor" or the abuser. Your abuser, however, as you so well know, can be very manipulative and believable. This same problem arises when law enforcement officers are called to the scene of a violent episode in a same-sex couple. Unless obvious injuries or witnesses are present, the officers may have difficulty distinguishing between abuser and victim and might be less likely to take appropriate action.

Same-sex abusers or abusers in transgender relationships have additional means of controlling and threatening their victims. One common controlling strategy is the threat of "outing" a partner who has not yet chosen to come out of the closet to certain groups. The threat may be to inform their partner's workplace, possibly risking job security. The threat may be to tell your landlord, which, in some states, may allow for eviction. As appalling as these actions sound, your abuser may have used the culture's built-in homophobia to control you.

Fear of Damaging Your Community

Just as the larger society in general holds many myths about abusive relationships, the gay and lesbian community has some ingrained myths of its own. Some in the gay, lesbian, and bisexual community believe that their community is characterized by harmony and mutual support. It is difficult for some within the gay, lesbian, and transgender culture to believe that intimate abuse and violence can exist in *all* intimate relationships and is not something unique to heterosexual couples. This false belief further isolates the survivors of same-sex abuse from even those who share their sexual orientation. When they do reach out for help from those who might seem most able to empathize and help, they may once again be met with disbelief and rejection.

On the other hand, for some same-sex abuse survivors one reason they may avoid reaching out for help to those outside the gay or lesbian community is because they fear further stigmatizing others. They fear that admitting the abuse, particularly to people outside their community, may create an additional excuse for a heterosexist world to label gay and lesbian relationships as abnormal or deviant. For this reason, some same-sex survivors feel that it is preferable to remain silent about their abuse.

Losses

As an abuse survivor from a gay, lesbian, or transgender relationship you may fear the possibility of losses in addition to those typically experienced by survivors from "traditional" heterosexual couples (see Chapter 7, "Losing Your Partner, Your Dream, Your Life"). As mentioned earlier, in states where no legal protections exist, many gay men, lesbians, or transgendered individuals risk losing their job or being evicted if their sexual orientation becomes known to their employer or landlord. Even now, after you are free of the abusive partner, the fear of these potential losses may prevent you from seeking help.

If you have children, you may have experienced another very real fear. The risk of losing your children when leaving an abusive same-sex relationship is even greater than for women in heterosexual relationships. Unfortunately, due to cultural attitudes about sexual orientation, courts are not always supportive of the victims and may take the children away. In an attempt to control you now, your ex-partner may continue to make this threat.

Getting Out

Unfortunately, just as for heterosexual female survivors, leaving *any* abusive relationship can be a difficult, dangerous time. What happens once those in abusive gay, lesbian, or transgender relationships finally manage to leave? Is the recovery process the same as it is for a woman who was being abused by a man? In many ways, it is. The concerns for people who escape heterosexual male-on-female abusive relationships often apply to you as well. You most likely will feel the same sense of fear, loss, depression, and anxiety discussed throughout this book. However, all of these issues may be exaggerated for you for very legitimate reasons.

All victims of abuse experience a sense of unreality and disbelief: "How could my partner have treated me this way?" "How could I have ended up in this situation?" "How could I have been so wrong about that person?" For those in the types of relationships discussed in this chapter, these reactions may be greatly heightened due to the societal myths, misconceptions, and prejudices discussed in the preceding section.

Once you identified the abuse you may also have recognized that a woman abuser or abuse in a same-sex or transgender relationship are not seen as the "norm" for abusive relationships. You may question yourself about how you formed a relationship with this person when there are so many other potential partners who are not abusive. You may begin to wonder if your choice of a partner reflects badly on you. Nothing could be further from the truth: Abuse in any relationship is never the victim's fault. Accepting this, however, may be even more difficult for some survivors.

If you were not able to find others to support and understand you and you experienced threats or violence, your sense of fear now may be even greater than for female survivors from opposite-sex relationships. The realization that friends, family, and the professionals charged with helping you, such as the police, the courts, and even crisis centers, may not completely understand your nontraditional abuse situation, increases your sense of isolation, and that can be very frightening.

Survivors of the forms of abuse discussed in this chapter may find the feeling of loss of support from family and friends and the feeling of losing the respect of colleagues are extra intense. Family, friends, and colleagues may see the idea of abuse in a relationship such as yours as a perfect opportunity for jokes, although these same people would never dream of making light of a female victim of a male abuser. If you stand up for yourself, they may brush you off as someone who "just can't take a joke."

In addition, the depression that often paradoxically follows escaping an abusive relationship may also be different. Rates of depression in the population overall are greater for women than for men; however, the number of suicides stemming from depression are greater for men. This may indicate that male survivors of female-on-male or male-on-male abuse who become depressed are more at risk of using more deadly methods for attempting to end their lives.

If the abuse you endured included sexual assault you may find it terribly difficult to seek or find help for recovering from this. Society often turns a blind eye to men as victims of sexual assault by women partners and to abuse in same-sex or transgender relationships. Some people still falsely believe that men cannot be sexually abused by women, and that sexual abuse in a same-sex relationship just "goes with the territory."

As you can see, some important differences and unique challenges do exist for female-on-male and gay, lesbian, or transgender abuse. You may analyze more deeply for yourself the unique challenges couples in diverse abusive relationships face by completing the Self-Exploration, "Your Unique Challenges," at the end of this chapter.

However, the diverse abusive relationships discussed in this chapter are more *similar* to, than different from opposite-sex, male-on-female abuse that is the primary focus of most of this book. Because of that similarity, *anyone* can be in an abusive or violent relationship, regardless of the sex of the abuser and of the victim.

Your Unique Challenges

As mentioned throughout this chapter, the difficulties faced by men abused by women or abuse by gay, lesbian, or transgender partners pose additional challenges in surviving and escaping the abuser. If you were in such a relationship, this exercise will help you become more aware of the difficulties you faced and may be trying to cope with still.

In each category below, explain briefly all the tactics or situations you can think of that your abuser used against you or ways in which others in society increased the pain and difficulties of your abusive experience.

- Your abuser, family, or friends (or you?) used stereotypical myths and stereotypes to deny the reality of the abuse.

_____

_____

_____

- Your abuser told you that no one would believe you because you were not a "traditional" victim.

_____

_____

_____

- Your abuser was able to mistreat you in public without repercussions.

_____

_____

_____

- If you were part of an abusive gay, lesbian, or transgender relationship, your abuser threatened to "out you"; to tell others about your relationship (your family, friends, employer, landlord, school) to keep you quiet about the abuse.

_____

_____

_____

- Your family or friends refused to acknowledge the nature of your relationship.

_____

_____

_____

- Your family or friends treated your abuse as a joke.

_____

_____

_____

- Your family or friends told you that the abuse was your fault. What were the suggestions (if any) they made to "stop" the abuse?

_____

_____

_____

- Outside agencies (therapists, law enforcement, etc.) talked as though only one type of relationship (heterosexual), abuser (male-on-female), and victim (female) exists.

_____

_____

_____

- Once told about your relationship, the counselor or social worker at the agency where you sought help acted surprised or shocked, or asked you inappropriate questions about your relationship.

Now review your list. This will help increase your understanding about why it was so difficult for you to survive and escape the abusive relationship you were in, and the intensity of your personal experience of relationship abuse or violence. That understanding, in turn, will help you focus on the areas of your life now that need the most attention for you to heal. Finding people and support agencies that can be truly empathetic and empowering to you is very important. Although it may take a bit more time for you to find the help you need, it will be worth the search (see the "Resources" section at the end of this book).

PART

II

Now

7
Losing Your Partner, Your Dream, Your Life

Myth: Losing an abusive partner isn't painful. It's a relief.

Myth: Dealing with the loss of an abusive relationship is much easier than losing a healthy relationship.

Whenever any relationship ends, most people experience pain. Even if the breakup was *your* idea, it can still hurt. After finally leaving your abuser, you might have been surprised that you felt sadness. Anticipating the relief you would feel to be out (and it *was* a relief), may have led you to believe it wouldn't be emotionally painful. The pain may not have surfaced for days, weeks, months, or sometimes even years after the relationship ended. But at some point it probably did.

If you are like most people who have left an abusive relationship, the sadness and loss you feel may be just as severe as if a healthy relationship had ended. The loss of an intimate relationship, even a bad one, involves pain on a number of levels. You have not just lost a partner, you have lost much more.

You Lost a Part of Yourself

Have you sensed that you are not the same person you were before the abuse? Survivors often talk about losing parts of their personalities. Friends and family may have mentioned to you how different you seem now. If you were outgoing, assertive, or carefree before the abuse, you may now act more withdrawn, passive, or rigid. Perhaps you detect other new characteristics in yourself such as excessive anger, pessimism, or a general distrust of others.

It's not difficult to understand how the trauma you experienced could be powerful enough to produce fundamental changes in who you are. These changes add to the list of losses you are mourning. Chances are good, however, that the real you has not been lost permanently. Over time you will begin to see glimpses of your old self: those healthy, positive traits will begin to reappear. Eventually, you will probably be able to recapture that person you used to be and used to love.

You Lost a Companion and Confidant

You may miss having someone to accompany you through daily highs and lows. No longer having someone to "mull" things over with at night or turn to for a second opinion about personal problems, finances, the children, daily activities, or whatever, may leave you feeling as if you have a "hole" in your life.

Moreover, when a relationship ends, you often lose someone who was, at least in some ways, a confidant. Regardless of the abuse, you may have talked with your ex-partner about things you didn't discuss with anyone else. You may have discussed personal, intimate issues. When the relationship ended, your confidant was gone.

Even though you know your decision to leave was the right one, you may experience loneliness. Losing the person you thought was a life partner leaves a large empty space in your life. This sorrow does not mean the relationship was healthy; you know it wasn't. Nor does it imply that you really wanted or needed to be in an abusive relationship; you know that's not true. It just means you feel the loss of some parts of your relationship.

You Lost Your Sexuality

If your sexual life with your partner was good, you probably miss the physical pleasure. Also, you may miss simply having a physically intimate relationship in your life: someone to hold you, to be physically near you, to kiss you hello or goodnight. You may miss holding someone's hand as you walk and sleeping next to someone at night.

On the other hand, however, you also lost your "sexual innocence." In this context, sexual innocence does not mean sexual inexperience or a naiveté about sex; it refers to feeling comfortable and trusting with a sexual partner. If your relationship was sexually abusive, you experienced a different kind of sexual loss: the loss of feeling like a sexually healthy person. Your abuser took control over your body and took your sexuality away from you. No one has the right to take that from another person.

If you feel you are mourning the loss of your sexual innocence, that's a perfectly normal reaction. That your body is your own and *you* determine if and how and when you will have sex was taken away from you. Your ex took away your ability to trust future potential intimate partners. He stole all of this from you and you have every right to mourn such a loss.

If your partner sexually assaulted you, your ability to feel sexual in a positive, loving way was probably taken away, too. It may be a long time before you begin to experience and feel comfortable with the sexual side of yourself again. Even when those feelings of sensuality and sexuality do return, you may experience great difficulty being sexual with your next partner. Intimacy with someone new may trigger memories and sensations of the horrors of the abuse. These thoughts may cause you to avoid sexual situations completely until you are able to move past those memories. This is a normal reaction to your abuse history and another reason to feel a sense of loss (refer to Chapter 17, "Loving Again").

An opposite reaction may sometimes occur for survivors of sexual abuse. Some survivors may become much more sexual with a greater number of partners than they ever would have before the abuse. This is probably a way for them to attempt to deal with the violence they experienced. They may be desperately trying to find a way to feel loved or whole again sexually. For others, the disgust toward their bodies may propel them into treating themselves as sexual objects. Unfortunately many women who take this path are hurt emotionally or even physically again.

You Lost Your Ability to Trust

If your abuser used discussions of issues such as finances, attitudes, or other activities as an excuse to ignite abusive episodes, you may be experiencing a very different sort of loss. If you were afraid to initiate discussions because of the potentially abusive results, you may still find yourself avoiding these discussions now with everyone. You may avoid talking to others, particularly a new partner, about anything that feels like an old abuse "trigger."

If the abuse has caused you to feel anxious about being open and direct with others, this is another very real loss. Your ability to be assertive and speak your mind without fear of violence is a terrible sacrifice. This may feel as though another very important part of you was stolen.

You Lost Your Life Dream

You also may be mourning the loss of a life dream. When you began the relationship, you may have felt that he was *the* one. You may have envisioned a life together forever. You might have planned to marry, have children, and grow old together. Now, you may feel a sense of great loss for the dream you once thought you shared.

You may have lost many other dreams along the way: your dreams of owning a home; living in a community as an intact, happy family; being in a long-term, secure relationship. You are mourning all these losses. Knowing it was the right decision to leave should not in any way diminish allowing yourself to grieve. You know now that your dream could never have become reality, but the loss makes you sad nonetheless.

If you had to move away to escape your abuser, it may have been necessary to leave your job. You may even have sacrificed your career. You worked hard to get where you were, to establish a good reputation at work, perhaps to advance up the ranks. After leaving your position, it may have been difficult for you to reestablish yourself in the work world. Being forced to start all over again in a new job can create profound feelings of loss.

You Lost Your Dreams for Children

If you envisioned a life with him that included children, but you did not have children together, you may be wondering when, if ever, you will have your family. Your experience of abuse may have altered your thoughts about having children at all in the future. Maybe you wisely chose not to bring children into such an abusive atmosphere, but now you wonder if you will ever feel comfortable enough in a relationship to have a family in the future. This may be another source of grief for you.

If you had children with your ex-partner or you had children from an earlier relationship, you probably assumed at the time that you were creating a happy, stable family. As the relationship turned to abuse, you may also be mourning the loss of a healthy upbringing for your children. One of the most difficult legacies of an abusive relationship can be the sense of loss you feel for your children; guilt at exposing them to your former partner for as long as you did. It is easy in hindsight to see what you might have done differently. But if leaving sooner had risked your safety or your children's, you did, without a doubt, what was best for them.

If your children witnessed the abuse you endured, you may now feel the loss of their innocence, too. If your former partner directly abused your children, you are grieving for that as well. No matter what the particulars were, if you believe that your children sacrificed parts of their childhood because of this abusive relationship, it makes perfect sense that you would mourn their losses. You believed that the relationship would provide a father for your children. This assumption was shattered by his abuse.

Sometimes a survivor has no choice but to leave the children behind to escape the violence with her own life. If this was true for you, your grief and loss are further magnified. But, you had to get away. Witnessing the abuse over and over may have been far more traumatic for your children than being separated from you temporarily (see Chapter 10, "What About the Children?"). If you had stayed, and your partner's violence escalated to extreme violence or murder, your children might have lost their mother forever. If you are not able to see or contact your children right now, chances are that you will find a way to be reunited with them, hopefully in the near future (see Chapter 12, "Practical Considerations").

You Lost Family and Friends

You probably lost other people in your life when you left your abuser. You may have developed close ties to some of your ex's family members, but now have no contact whatsoever. There probably were mutual friends, but they either did not know or refused to believe you about the abuse. They may have remained loyal to your abuser and deserted you when the relationship ended. And, if you needed to hide from your former partner, that meant hiding from them, too. You may have lost everyone.

Think back for a moment about how your family and friends reacted when your relationship ended. If they were not understanding and supportive, you may have lost them, too. Perhaps they failed to support you because they refused to believe the abuse was occurring, because they felt that it was your duty to stay with your partner, or perhaps they even blamed *you*. Their reactions and attitudes probably eliminate any possibility for you to feel close to them now. They may have thought they were being supportive, but their actions and words were not helpful. So, you may have chosen, wisely, to separate yourself from them (see Chapter 11, "The Reactions of Others"). Even if the distancing was *your* decision, you feel that loss.

You Lost Your Valued Possessions

During your relationship your ex-partner may have damaged or destroyed some of your most treasured personal belongings. Often, an abuser will destroy, sell, or toss out specific possessions knowing you prize them the most. You may have lost some irreplaceable items that had great sentimental value for you. This is one more weapon in your abuser's arsenal of control and manipulation. He may have smashed objects during violent episodes, or you may have noticed items broken or missing when you returned home "too late" or following an evening out with friends of whom your ex didn't "approve." In addition, when you left your abuser, it's possible you had to abandon many valued personal effects.

If you and your partner shared expenses, such as mortgage payments or rent, utilities, food, or car payments, or if your abuser brought in most or all of the family income, you lost a large part of your economic security as well. Often such a loss can make you feel insecure and unsafe.

It is natural to mourn these losses. Although your treasures can never be replaced, you now are able to protect the cherished belongings in your life. You can be confident that no one will be able to take them from you again.

The Pain of Loss

After considering all the possible reasons *why* you may be grieving, it is important to examine what this grieving feels like. Elisabeth Kübler-Ross, the famous researcher on loss, grief, and death, discussed in her book, *On Death and Dying*, the stages experienced by someone who is dying or has lost a loved one. These stages can be adapted to the loss you experienced when your relationship ended.

Kübler-Ross's stages of grieving do not always follow a predictable pattern. This is particularly true if you are grieving the loss of an abusive relationship. Your loss is very complicated and may alter not only the pattern of the stages but the length, intensity, and sequencing of each stage.

The first stage discussed by Kübler-Ross is shock or *denial*. Even though you may have been planning the demise of your relationship for a long time, it may seem unreal when it finally happens. It can take a while before waking up in the morning with the clear realization that you are out. You may find you maintain patterns of behavior as if you are still in the relationship. Eventually, however, this denial will disappear.

Another stage of loss you probably experienced was *anger*. It is much safer to allow yourself to feel your anger when you are free of the danger of the relationship. If you had allowed yourself to feel this anger while you were together, you may have created greater risk. Submitting to your partner's demands would have become unbearable if your anger surfaced. And not submitting may have made him far more dangerous. Now that you are out, you can allow yourself to feel the anger. But instead of feeling anger about a single, recent episode of violence, you may now feel all your anger rise up at once (see Chapter 8, "When Feelings Overwhelm You"). Some of this anger may be directed at yourself. You may blame yourself for allowing such a relationship to happen to you, for not leaving sooner, for not standing up for yourself. These are perfectly normal feelings, but try to keep in mind that you did the best you could to survive.

Depression is another stage in the grieving process. Sadness, tearfulness, disrupted sleep patterns, and poor concentration are signs of the depression that often appears after the end of an abusive relationship. These symptoms may progress into a deeper, more profound depression. Again, this is a normal reaction to the abuse and there are ways of treating your depression (see Chapter 13, "Beginning to Heal").

Finally, gradually, over many months and perhaps years, you may come to the stage of grieving called *acceptance*. This doesn't simply mean accepting that the relationship is over. It means you no longer are reacting to the abuse as if it were still part of your daily life. It means you have worked through the pain this relationship left you with and are beginning to move on. Even if this seems impossible to you right now, it will happen. It may not happen easily or quickly, but at some time in the future the abuse will no longer be such a powerfully painful part of your everyday life.

Coping with the Losses

Overcoming loss is a slow process. One of the worst things you can do is to hurry it. Many others may expect you to "cheer up and be happy" and get on with life. They will say things like, "You should be feeling great—you're out!" But they are only seeing that you got out of a bad relationship. They are not in a position to see all the related losses that you are suffering.

Only you know the healing you have to do and how long it will take. If you are worrying that the grieving process is going on too long, think about how long you loved and believed in your partner. If you were together for years, then believing the pain should be over in a few weeks or a month is unrealistic. If you rush your healing, you might end up burying the pain, only to find it resurfacing in the future.

You need to allow yourself to feel bad. If you have one of those days when you are tearful all day, that's OK. Crying is not a sign of weakness, and it's not silly. It means that you are allowing yourself to *feel*. Until you allow yourself to experience the emotions of that loss, you can't begin the healing process.

It best not to try to go through this alone. Find someone you can talk to about how you are feeling. Make sure it is someone who is going to listen without judging you. That person should be someone who can recognize that, no matter how abusive the relationship was, there are still many losses you must mourn. He or she must be willing to stick with you through your grieving and not try to hurry you. This could be a good friend, a close family member, a therapist, someone from your church, or anyone you feel you can trust to listen to and hear you.

Often in abusive relationships, many things are left unsaid. You probably weren't able to tell your ex-partner everything you would like to say. You may have stayed silent because of the potential for further abuse or because your feelings fell on deaf ears. It's important to be able to vent your feelings even if you can't do so face-to-face with your abuser (see the *Self-Exploration* exercise at the end of this chapter).

Reading books, articles, and Internet sites about loss can help. This is another means of "sharing" your feelings with others. Reading about others who have gone through what you are experiencing can make you feel less alone with your pain (see Resources).

Meeting with a counselor or therapist who understands how painful and difficult this healing process is for you can help, too. With a counselor's guidance, you may be able to allow yourself to grieve without judgment or self-recrimination. Venting to someone else about your pain can, all by itself, help you to heal (see Chapter 13, "Beginning to Heal").

You probably have not been able to tell your abuser how you feel about how you were treated. Releasing some of those feelings can be a very therapeutic experience.

For this exercise, set aside about an hour (or more if you think you need it). In the space at the end of the exercise (and on as many more sheets of paper as you need) write a letter to your abuser. You will *not* send this letter, so feel free to write everything you have ever wanted to say to your ex-partner. Take your time. There is no right or wrong way to do this, no right or wrong words to use. The list below offers some suggestions for thoughts you might want to include in your letter. Feel free to use it as a guideline or write it in your own words if that feels more comfortable.

Dear [your abuser] _____,

1. **What is your purpose in writing this letter?**
2. **How did your abuser make you feel?**
3. **What losses have you endured that were your abuser's fault?**
4. **What other feelings such as shock, anger, or depression are you experiencing, what are they like, and how did your abuser cause them?**
5. **What else would you like to say about your abuser and the abuse you suffered?**

When you are done with your letter, set it aside. Put it in a place where you won't see it on a daily basis. Then begin to pay attention to any new thoughts that you wish you could have said to your ex-partner. When these thoughts occur, get the letter out and add them to it. Keep adding to your letter until you find that at least one week passes without feeling the need to make any new additions.

The next step is to decide what to do with your letter. If you find that you are not ready to part with it, that's OK. Put it away until you decide it is time to get it out of your life.

When you decide it's time, make a ritual out of the destroying of the letter. Think about what would feel right to you: ripping it up into a million little pieces, burying it, burning it, or some combination of these. Decide if you want to do this alone or accompanied by a trusted friend. Do not be surprised by your reactions when you destroy the letter: relief, anger, satisfaction, sadness, or virtually any other emotions are all possible and normal.

Finally, if this exercise seemed helpful, and more thoughts and feelings emerge over time, repeat the process. As always, there is no right or wrong way to do it, but hopefully you will find this exercise very therapeutic.

8

When Feelings Overwhelm You

Myth: The emotional turmoil you experience in the aftermath of an abusive relationship is brief and usually fairly mild.

Myth: All survivors experience very similar emotions after leaving an abusive relationship.

*I*t's easy to imagine that some of the strong emotions such as fear, anxiety, anger, and depression that accompany an abusive relationship would immediately subside when you are finally away from your abuser. Yet nothing could be further from the truth. Many of those debilitating feelings can linger for months or even years, and new undesirable emotions may appear in the aftermath of the abuse.

Healing requires you to understand that these ongoing feelings are normal and will diminish over time, either through your own efforts or, in some cases, with outside help such as counseling or therapy. Although every abused person's emotional struggles will be different, here are some of the most common and often most difficult feelings.

Fear

Removing yourself from your abuser does not mean that all your fear simply disappears. Many people who have escaped violent partners know the danger may follow them beyond the relationship. *You* are the best judge of how safe you are. Be sure to read Chapter 2 ("Are You Out of Danger Now?"), and take whatever steps are necessary to increase your safety.

Many people have difficulty understanding why you are still afraid *after* the relationship ends. But, you know all too well that your partner may not stop the abuse and violence just because you left. In fact, it might escalate. You know your ex was not always "rational." Even if it means risking arrest and jail by violating a restraining order, he may still try to hurt you. So, it is *perfectly normal* for you to continue to be afraid.

Your abuser may not have overtly threatened or attempted to kill you, but nevertheless, you may have been in a nearly constant state of terror. When a partner acts irrationally and impulsively, it becomes impossible to predict what might happen next. If the abuse in your relationship slowly intensified over time, the logical assumption you made was that it would continue to increase. Remember, your abuser did so many unbelievable things to you. How could you *not* live in fear of all the other unimaginable acts of which he was capable?

What if you know, intellectually, there is no reason for you to be fearful now, and yet you are still afraid? Perhaps your abuser has no way of finding you. Maybe he's in jail. Maybe you have moved and your ex has no way of finding you. You *know*, at least for now, that you are not in any real danger. However, many reasons exist for your fear.

Chances are you lived with fear in your relationship for a long time. The fear you experienced may not have been based solely on the threat of being killed. It may have been the fear of physical, verbal, or emotional assault. Fear may have become a "normal" part of your very "not normal" daily life.

Now that you are out of that abusive situation, do you continue to experience fear when an event occurs that used to "set him off"? Even common, daily occurrences may activate this terrible downward spiral. Now that you are out, these daily events don't lead to abuse, but your mind and body have been conditioned to associate them with the aggression. So, when one of these triggers occurs, your *automatic* emotional and physical response is fear. Keep in mind, it took time for this fear to be conditioned in you and it may take almost as long for you to "unlearn" those associations. Just as you learned these defense mechanisms gradually, you will unlearn them gradually as well.

Guilt

You know the abuse wasn't your fault. You know you did everything you could to prevent and, finally, to end the abuse. You know you did what was necessary to survive that relationship. You didn't do anything wrong! *So, why do you still feel guilty?*

Guilt is one of those very sneaky emotions. Intellectually, you know you have no reason to feel guilty and yet, there it is. You can tell yourself the guilt will do you no good, but it persists. Experiencing guilt after leaving an abusive relationship can be one of the most confusing emotions.

So, again, why is it you feel guilty? The best way to understand this is to determine the source of your original guilt. Usually, the "bait" for your guilt was set before the relationship even began.

Do you remember your abuser using subtle forms of guilt to get you into the relationship at the very beginning? These tactics may have included complaining you were unfair to refuse to go out with him or telling you how painful it felt when you refused him. Can you remember how you began to feel you were doing something *wrong* if you didn't begin a relationship with him?

Once you did get into the relationship, the use of guilt increased. If you didn't want to do what he wanted, when he wanted to do it, he made you feel you had done something *wrong*. Anytime you had a difference of opinion, your ex found a way to leave you feeling your opinion was *wrong* and you were *wrong* to have disagreed with him. Your abuser may have reinforced this guilt by telling you how much he loved you and only wanted what was best for you. If you resisted or disagreed with him, your ex claimed you were hurting him deeply and you just didn't understand the true depths of his love.

Guilt was a very powerful tool for seizing control over you. Your abuser won a major battle when he established a pattern of making you feel at fault whenever you disagreed or opposed him in any way. Think back on the relationship. Do you remember feeling at fault and guilty whenever problems arose in the relationship? Do you remember feeling guilty even when you knew it was in no way your fault? These feelings become ingrained and do not simply evaporate when you are free of the relationship.

Your abuser may have blamed you for situations that were obviously no one's fault. This may have happened when circumstances were beyond anyone's control: the car broke down, the toilet backed up, the kids got sick. Although you were in no way responsible for these occurrences, you still got blamed. Not only was the "problem" blamed on you, the abuse that often followed was blamed on you as well.

You may have been blamed for things that did not even exist. A common example of this is the extreme jealousy abusers often exhibit. If your partner was excessively jealous, he may have blamed and abused you for nonexistent flirting or just talking with others. Again, you were made to feel guilty when you had done nothing wrong.

Finally, guilt was heaped on you for the fact that the abuse continued. How often after an abusive episode did you hear, "I'm sorry, but if only you hadn't..." This was the ultimate guilt tactic—*making you responsible for your own abuse*—and therefore you felt it was your fault.

When guilt is so deeply instilled in you, whether it stems solely from this abusive relationship or grows out of other experiences from your life as well, it is difficult to let it go. It takes time to get past the guilt, no matter how vicious and traumatic the abuse you endured. Now that you are out, you may find it easy to take on new guilt. You may find yourself thinking, "If only I hadn't..." Hindsight can be painful, especially when it involves berating yourself for actions you couldn't control. The more you heal from the abuse, the easier it will be to release yourself from your guilt.

Impulsivity

Many people who manage to escape abusive relationships feel an overwhelming impulse to change everything about their lives all at once. They may feel as if the only way to recover is to put the past totally out of their mind and to make everything somehow "new." Your desire for a new life may be so strong that you are motivated to change jobs, living arrangements, and even your friends without really giving these important decisions the thought they deserve.

Although moving on in your life after an abusive relationship is indeed very important, if you move too fast you may later regret some of the choices you made in a time of extreme emotional crisis. You have the opportunity to find out what you really want and need, and you should consider taking some time to make the best decisions you can for your future.

This may seem paradoxical, but freeing yourself from an abusive or violent relationship is, for most survivors, a far more emotionally complex task than getting into one. In fact, many of you, as you look back, may remember that you became intimately involved with your abusive partner very quickly (most likely, *too* quickly, at his insistence; see Chapter 17, "Loving Again," for more about this process). Consequently, it makes a great deal of sense to expect the post-relationship adjustment period to require more time and emotional effort on your part. As with any pain in our lives, we want it to end as fast as possible. In this case, however, it's usually far healthier and more healing to *give it time*.

Unreleased Anger

What about the anger you feel? Is your anger still buried although it's been weeks, months, or years since your abusive relationship ended? Perhaps others have asked you why you don't appear angry with your abuser. People may have even encouraged you to "let your anger out"! It makes perfect sense to be angry, enraged even, after getting out, but you just don't seem to feel it. The truth may be that you just don't feel it *yet*. Your outward indifference to what he did to you may end one of these days and you may explode with rage.

This is normal. You concealed your anger for so long, it may take months or years before you are ready to express it fully. You may be afraid of fully releasing your anger, of losing control over these strong emotions. Hiding your anger was a defense mechanism that served you well with your abuser. It was one of many strategies you used to survive in that relationship. After a while it became routine. You may have learned this "trick" so well, unlearning it now is difficult.

What do you think would happen if you were to release all your anger? Are you afraid the anger will somehow overpower you if you allow it to escape? Or are you worried you may never be able to move past it? Once you begin to express the anger it may feel somewhat overwhelming for a while, but you *will* move beyond it. Your anger will not destroy you (see the next section, "Anger Released"). If you are truly afraid or unable to release your anger, you may need to work with a counselor to help you feel safe enough to express these most powerful emotions.

Some people are afraid that if they release their anger, it will be directed at people who don't deserve it. However, those who know you and are aware of your past know that anger is a normal reaction to the abuse. If you were to express your anger, and some of it was misdirected toward them, they would probably understand, support you, and even feel relieved that your emotions were finally emerging. If you find that some misplaced anger upsets friends or family members, talk to them afterward about what happened. Apologize and explain that you are still working through some of your emotions from the abuse and your anger was not directed at them. Being open and honest with them should help to smooth out any hurt feelings.

Remember, good friends will not abandon you, or judge you for doing something you need to do: release your pent-up emotions. If your anger surfaces often or becomes too intense for your friendships and other relationships to bear, then it may be time to think about getting outside help. Chapter 13, "Beginning to Heal," can assist you in finding outside support.

Anger Released

For some of you, once you were out and safe, all of that stored-up anger may have exploded all at once. For many people, when that stockpile of stored anger begins to erupt, "capping" it may be difficult or impossible. Anger may have controlled your life for so long that now you find it difficult to feel anything except rage.

Anger directed at your abuser is, of course, one of the most normal reactions a person can have. But as with any emotion, anger can sometimes rise to excessive levels. You may have been so angry you wanted to hurt your abuser back, just as he hurt you. Perhaps you even have elaborate fantasies about strategies for exacting emotional and physical vengeance.

Thoughts of hurting your abuser are not wrong or dangerous in themselves. Thoughts are nothing more than that: thoughts. Most survivors have such fantasies at one time or another. But, if you suspect you may act on your fantasies (such as through criminal acts, behaviors that could jeopardize child custody decisions, actions that might risk direct retaliation from him, etc.), safer and more effective ways exist to release your anger (see Chapter 13, "Beginning to Heal").

Depression

Since you left your abuser, have you felt very down, sad, or fatigued for no obvious reason? Have your eating and sleeping patterns changed significantly? Do you feel your situation in life is hopeless? Do you feel helpless? Have you lost interest in your favorite activities? These are among the most common signs and symptoms of depression.

Depression is the most universal emotional experience for survivors of an abusive relationship. Once you are out and relatively safe, you can contemplate the relationship in ways that weren't possible when you were in it. Although, in the long run, you may find such reflection to be desirable and helpful in your healing process, it can also create a great sense of sadness and loss.

As mentioned in Chapter 7, "Losing Your Partner, Your Dream, Your Life," you suffered many losses because of the abuse. These losses create great sadness and often serious depression similar to the experience of loss we feel when a loved one dies. It is difficult to imagine how anyone could experience what you did and not feel profound sadness and sorrow. Grief and depression over your losses are perfectly normal. But severe depression can be terribly debilitating and can create barriers to your healing process. So, it's important for you to be aware of depression's signs and symptoms.

Some signs that are relatively easy to spot involve major changes in your daily habits. If your eating pattern has changed and you find yourself seriously overeating or undereating, this could be a symptom of depression. The same is true for your sleeping habits. Depression is frequently characterized by insomnia, difficulty falling asleep, frequent awakenings during the night, waking in the early morning and being unable to go back to sleep, or a combination of these symptoms. On the other hand, you may find that you are sleeping considerably more than usual. And though your amount of sleep is far greater than before, you find you always feel exhausted. Sleep may have become a welcome escape from the echoes of the abuse, but it's also a frequent sign of depression.

Other common indicators of depression are feelings of hopelessness, overwhelming sadness, a belief that your life will never improve, thoughts that you really don't deserve better, and, most disturbing, thoughts of hurting or killing yourself.

Look at any history of depression in your life in the past. If you exhibited a pattern of depression before the abusive relationship, be sure to consider that you may be more prone to it now. It is possible your depression may go deeper than your current healing process. Remember, depression may be situational and temporary as you deal with the abuse you suffered, or it may be a more persistent chemical imbalance in your brain. Preexisting depression, especially if it has been characteristic of your life in the past, might be a medical condition that you need to discuss with your doctor or a therapist to determine appropriate treatment, including the possibility of medication.

Although it is difficult for anyone to say exactly how long is "too long" for depression to last following an abusive relationship, you can examine the course of your depression for clues to how you are doing. Do you feel worse than you did a month or two ago? Is the depression beginning to interfere with your relationships with others, your job, or other parts of your daily life? Are you increasingly unable to accomplish the everyday tasks of life? Overall, do you feel that your mood is not improving? Improvement, by itself, does not imply that your depression is gone. It means you can now identify minutes, hours, or perhaps days when you feel less depressed than last week or last month. If you feel you are becoming less depressed, that your depression is decreasing in frequency and duration, you are probably on the right track, but you still want to be attentive to your moods.

The most important time to be concerned about depression is when your depressed moods are accompanied by thoughts of killing yourself. The fear, anger, and depression that surface in the aftermath of the abuse can make you feel so terrible you just don't want to face them. Your abuser made you feel so terrible for so long, the pain may be just too great to accept. This is especially true if you believed your life would be instantly transformed when you left him. Now, the reality of this difficult time of transition and the amount of work still to do may feel overwhelmingly oppressive and hopeless. Those feelings can turn a depressed person into a suicidal one.

If you are having thoughts of suicide, *get help*. Talk to your physician or a therapist or call a suicide prevention line where you can remain anonymous it you want. As difficult as it may be to believe now, things *will* get better. It takes time for your emotions to surface and run their course. You've accomplished a great deal—giving up now is simply shortchanging yourself. You deserve to live a happy, abuse-free life. It *can* happen. It will just take time (see Chapter 13, "Beginning to Heal"). Consider finding someone supportive to help you through this difficult time. You shouldn't feel hesitant or embarrassed about talking with a therapist. Again, your feelings are justified. Allowing someone to help you shows great inner strength and courage. Friends and family members can probably listen and offer support, but they are not trained professionally to help you through your depression. Calling on professionals for this help is the greatest stride you can take toward healing.

Anger Turned Inward: Self-Injurious Behavior

Following an abusive relationship, some survivors find that they have an overpowering urge to hurt *themselves*. This feeling can be one of the most difficult to admit to anyone. If you have felt this way and have shared these feelings with others, their responses may not have been as supportive or helpful as you had hoped. They were probably shocked or disbelieving. They may have expressed to you their feeling that you endured enough pain and violence in your relationship, so you must be crazy to hurt yourself more now that you are free of the abuse.

You are *not* crazy. Victims of abuse physically hurt themselves for a number of psychological reasons. Many survivors say they experience a period of emotional numbness. It is frightening to feel nothing at all and even scarier to think you may never feel anything ever again. Numbness is an effective defense mechanism that helps to keep emotions from overwhelming you. Hurting yourself (cutting, scratching, burning, etc.) may be a way of testing your senses and reassuring yourself that you can indeed "feel" something. Feelings will come back to you in time. The numbness will eventually subside. You may not be ready to experience the full force of your emotions yet.

Another reason for self-harm is an attempt to regain some control over your body and life. For so long, your abuser exerted control over your body. Strategies for this may have included objectifying you, making degrading comments about your appearance, sexual assault, or rape. He also controlled other aspects of your life: where you went, who you saw, what you did. Self-injurious behaviors may be your way of reclaiming the personal control you lost.

Some survivors of violent relationships develop a learned association between anxiety and pain. In your relationship, tension and anxiety usually preceded the violent episodes. Now that you are out, you may still have a strong mental connection between anxiety and pain. In your relationship, waiting for the violence to happen was, at times, unbearable. There still may be the desire to get the anxiety or fear "over and done with."

Your abuser went to great lengths to convince you of what a bad person you are. It may take you some time to let go of your negative self-concepts stemming from those actions. Injuring yourself may serve, in your mind, to prove how bad you are.

Whatever the reasons for hurting yourself, you may feel too embarrassed or ashamed to admit it to anyone. If you wish to deal with these feelings and behaviors, you may need to work with a counselor who is specifically trained in working with self-injurious behaviors. This counselor will not judge you or think you are crazy. He or she will work with you to recognize the origins of the behavior and help you deal with it.

Post-Traumatic Stress Disorder

If you lived through a particularly abusive relationship, you may suffer from post-traumatic stress disorder (PTSD; see Chapter 4 for more information about this).

Psychologists have found that veterans of wars are not the only group vulnerable to PTSD. Anyone who lives through any major trauma may suffer from PTSD. Does it seem to you that you lived through your own personal war? Was there a reason to be afraid a great deal of the time? Was life continually unpredictable with negative consequences no matter what you did? Did you experience abuse and violence that no person should ever have to endure? These events are very traumatic.

A common symptom of PTSD is to react more fearfully than others to startling events. When something alarming suddenly occurs, PTSD sufferers experience extreme responses such as heart palpitations, rapid breathing, and profuse sweating. Another characteristic of PTSD is the ominous feeling that something terrible is about to happen, although no real danger threat exists. Finally, if you are suffering from PTSD, you may find thoughts and images of the abuse suddenly jumping into your head for no reason. These images seem real, almost as if you are reliving them.

If you find that you are experiencing some of these symptoms, you may be suffering from PTSD. This doesn't mean that you are crazy or weak. It means you are having a normal reaction to a very abnormal ordeal in your life. When you stop to think about it, unfortunately many parallels exist between war and domestic violence. As with other emotions discussed in this chapter, PTSD symptoms will take time to subside. If you find that these symptoms are seriously interfering with your daily life, you may need to work with a counselor to overcome them.

Other Intense Emotions

The specific feelings addressed in this chapter are shared by many people who have endured and survived an abusive or violent relationship. It is by no means an exhaustive list of the many potential emotions that may be causing difficulty for you now. These powerful emotions are normal, predictable reactions to a terribly powerful episode in your life. Becoming aware of your emotions, giving yourself time to feel them, and finding the help you may need to deal with them will allow you to move beyond your self-defeating emotions to the healing and positive feelings you deserve.

Assessing Your Feelings

Sometimes survivors find it very difficult to assess their emotional difficulties. They also have difficulty being objective about the extent to which their feelings are interfering with their life. If you push your feelings aside or try to minimize them, you risk becoming stuck in them.

Note: This is a **weeklong** *Self-Exploration* exercise. It takes time and effort, so plan carefully and try to follow through with it. You will find it very helpful. If working on this exercise feels uncomfortable and anxiety-producing, you may need either to wait until you feel ready, or enlist the help of a counselor to support you while you explore your feelings.

- In Part I, check all of the feelings that you are experiencing.
- In Part II, document how often you are aware of the feelings during one week.
- In Part III, use the scale to determine how disturbing and disruptive the feelings are at different times during the day. As you complete the first three parts, also work on the last section of the chart.
- In Part IV, record each time your feelings of fear, anger, guilt, or depression interfere with your life. Do not judge your feelings. No "right or wrong" feelings exist. This chart is simply a way for you to examine your feelings more closely.

This exercise is designed to be repeated after one month and then again in six months so you can be aware of your progress. Over time you may well see decreases in number, frequency, severity, and effects of your destructive emotional responses. If such decreases take place, that means you're on the right track in your process of emotional healing. If your emotional responses stay about the same, but are not interfering too greatly with your daily life, maybe it will just take more time for you to move past them. If, however, you find that the number, frequency, or severity are increasing, you may want to consider some professional counseling to help you establish more effective management of your emotions so you can get on with the healing process.

Part I

Check the feelings you are experiencing. Check all that apply to you.

_____ Fear of continued violence by ex-partner

_____ Fear of violence by another person

_____ Other fear _____

_____ Anger toward ex-partner

_____ Anger toward yourself

_____ Anger over circumstances that contributed to the abuse

_____ Anger toward others who did not help

_____ Anger toward others not related to abuse

_____ Anger over current problems not associated with the abuse

_____ Other anger _____

_____ Guilt over having begun the relationship

_____ Guilt for having stayed in the relationship for as long as
you did

_____ Guilt about not being able to have ended your
partner's abuse

_____ Other guilt _____

_____ Feelings of sadness

_____ Feelings of hopelessness

_____ Change in eating pattern

_____ Change in sleeping pattern

_____ Thoughts of killing yourself

_____ Other related feelings of depression

_____ Thoughts of, or actual, cutting or other self-injury

_____ Extreme reaction to sudden sounds or events

_____ Thoughts of the abuse that suddenly jump into your mind

_____ Complete refusal to think about the abuse

_____ Other _____

_____ Other _____

Total number of items checked _____

Part II

For one week, note approximately how many times each of the feelings occurs.

Feeling	Days Experienced (Check All That Apply)						
	MON	TUES	WED	THURS	FRI	SAT	SUN
Fear of continued violence by ex-partner	—	—	—	—	—	—	—
Fear of violence by another person	—	—	—	—	—	—	—
Other fear _____	—	—	—	—	—	—	—
Anger toward ex-partner	—	—	—	—	—	—	—
Anger toward yourself	—	—	—	—	—	—	—
Anger over circumstances that contributed to the abuse	—	—	—	—	—	—	—
Anger toward others who did not help	—	—	—	—	—	—	—
Anger toward others not related to abuse	—	—	—	—	—	—	—
Anger over current problems not associated with the abuse	—	—	—	—	—	—	—
Other anger _____	—	—	—	—	—	—	—
Guilt over having begun the relationship	—	—	—	—	—	—	—
Guilt for having stayed in the relationship for as long as you did	—	—	—	—	—	—	—
Guilt about not being able to stop your partner's abuse	—	—	—	—	—	—	—
Other guilt _____	—	—	—	—	—	—	—
Feelings of sadness	—	—	—	—	—	—	—
Feelings of hopelessness	—	—	—	—	—	—	—

	MON	TUES	WED	THURS	FRI	SAT	SUN
Change in eating pattern	—	—	—	—	—	—	—
Change in sleeping pattern	—	—	—	—	—	—	—
Thoughts of killing yourself	—	—	—	—	—	—	—
Other related feelings of depression	—	—	—	—	—	—	—
Thoughts of, or actual, cutting or other self-injury	—	—	—	—	—	—	—
Extreme reaction to sudden sounds or events	—	—	—	—	—	—	—
Thoughts of the abuse that suddenly jump into your mind	—	—	—	—	—	—	—
Complete refusal to think about the abuse	—	—	—	—	—	—	—
Other _____							
_____	—	—	—	—	—	—	—
Other _____							
_____	—	—	—	—	—	—	—

Number of feelings experienced every day of the week _____

Number of feelings experienced 4 to 6 days during the week _____

Number of feelings experienced only 1 to 3 days during the week ___

Number of days free of any of these negative feelings _____

Part III

For each day, rate the severity of your feelings on a scale from 0 to 10, where 0 means the feeling did not occur at all that day, and 10 means that the feeling was the most powerful and consuming you can imagine.

Feeling	Severity Rating (0–10)						
	MON	TUES	WED	THURS	FRI	SAT	SUN
Fear of continued violence by ex-partner	__	__	__	__	__	__	__
Fear of violence by another person	__	__	__	__	__	__	__
Other fear _____	__	__	__	__	__	__	__
Anger toward ex-partner	__	__	__	__	__	__	__
Anger toward yourself	__	__	__	__	__	__	__
Anger over circumstances that contributed to the abuse	__	__	__	__	__	__	__
Anger toward others who did not help	__	__	__	__	__	__	__
Anger toward others not related to abuse	__	__	__	__	__	__	__
Anger over current problems not associated with the abuse	__	__	__	__	__	__	__
Other anger _____	__	__	__	__	__	__	__
Guilt over having begun the relationship	__	__	__	__	__	__	__
Guilt for having stayed in the relationship for as long as you did	__	__	__	__	__	__	__
Guilt about not being able to stop your partner's abuse	__	__	__	__	__	__	__
Other guilt _____	__	__	__	__	__	__	__
Feelings of sadness	__	__	__	__	__	__	__

	MON	TUES	WED	THURS	FRI	SAT	SUN
Feelings of hopelessness	—	—	—	—	—	—	—
Change in eating pattern	—	—	—	—	—	—	—
Change in sleeping pattern	—	—	—	—	—	—	—
Thoughts of killing yourself	—	—	—	—	—	—	—
Other related feelings of depression	—	—	—	—	—	—	—
Thoughts of, or actual, cutting or other self-injury	—	—	—	—	—	—	—
Extreme reaction to sudden sounds or events	—	—	—	—	—	—	—
Thoughts of the abuse that suddenly jump into your mind	—	—	—	—	—	—	—
Complete refusal to think about the abuse	—	—	—	—	—	—	—
Other _____	—	—	—	—	—	—	—
_____							
Other _____	—	—	—	—	—	—	—
_____							

Number of feelings rated over 8 _____

Number of feelings rated from 5 to 7 _____

Number of feelings rated from 2 to 4 _____

Number of feelings rated less than 2_____

Part IV

For each day, record the feelings you experienced and how each one affected your other emotions, attitudes, behaviors, and interactions with others.

Monday Feeling _____ Effect _____

     Feeling _____ Effect _____

     Feeling _____ Effect _____

Tuesday Feeling _____ Effect _____

     Feeling _____ Effect _____

     Feeling _____ Effect _____

Wednesday Feeling _____ Effect _____

     Feeling _____ Effect _____

     Feeling _____ Effect _____

Thursday Feeling _____ Effect _____

     Feeling _____ Effect _____

     Feeling _____ Effect _____

Friday Feeling _____ Effect _____

     Feeling _____ Effect _____

     Feeling _____ Effect _____

Saturday Feeling _____ Effect _____

     Feeling _____ Effect _____

     Feeling _____ Effect _____

Sunday Feeling _____ Effect _____

     Feeling _____ Effect _____

     Feeling _____ Effect _____

Remember, give your healing process about a month and then complete this exercise again. Then do so again after about six months. You will probably notice a steady decline in the power these negative emotions hold over you as you heal and become stronger with time.

9

Signs of Unfinished Healing

Myth: Once the abuse is in your past, you will quickly begin to feel good about yourself.

Myth: The end of an abusive relationship marks the beginning of new close and healthy relationships.

Myth: Your life and your attitudes will improve steadily and rapidly in the aftermath of an abusive relationship.

*T*his chapter offers you an opportunity to assess how well you are healing. It would be great if your self-esteem, emotional well-being, and relationships with others all bounced right back, but that doesn't usually happen. You will have good days and bad days, good weeks and bad weeks, good times and bad times. This doesn't mean that you are doing something wrong or you're a "slow healer": It's normal. All survivors heal at their own individual pace. No one heals overnight. Let's look more closely at the process of healing from an abusive relationship.

Look at the Big Picture

First, make sure you have realistic expectations. You do not need to have any deadlines or schedules. You just need to know you are heading in the right direction *overall*. If you feel you are doing better than you were a month or two ago, that's great. However, if your life is not improving or you perceive that you are feeling worse, that may be a signal to think about evaluating your progress toward healing.

You probably believed once you freed yourself from that awful relationship, life would quickly improve: no more frightening unpredictability; no more unwanted surprises; no more fear. Now, you may be realizing that life is not as predictable as you had hoped. You are not always sure how you will feel when you wake up in the morning, how you will make it through the day, how you will relate to others.

Many survivors expect a smooth, constant emotional upward swing after an abusive relationship is over. They expect each day to be better than the one before. When this doesn't happen, they may become discouraged, disheartened, and fearful that they may never feel better.

You probably notice some days are better than the day before. But, you also have those days when you seem to be in a holding pattern: not worse, but not better. Then, there are some days when you sink to what feels like new emotional lows. It's important for you to resist making these daily judgments about your life. It's much more helpful to look at your overall pattern of healing—like a graph with ups and downs, but moving overall upward. Healing is what's important, not how fast it happens.

Emotional Signs: Self-Esteem

Think back to your life before the relationship. If you had other abusive relationships before, try to think back to your life before the first one. Try to remember how you felt about yourself. If you were abused as a child, you may not have a time "before abuse." If that's the case, you may need to assess how your self-esteem has changed over the years as opposed to a "before and after." Did you believe you deserved respect? Did you assume you would find someone who would love you and treat you as well as you treated him? Did you see yourself as intelligent, attractive, sensitive, and caring? Did you feel you were able to love someone else fully? Did you believe you had talents and skills? Did you see yourself as a *worthy* person?

How do you perceive yourself now? Do you still hold yourself in high esteem? Do you believe you are capable of reaching your goals and enjoying a rewarding and fulfilling relationship? If not, it's time to evaluate how your abusive relationship sabotaged your self-esteem. Everyone deserves a positive and healthy self-image. You should be able to believe in yourself completely, and know that you deserve nothing but the best.

You can evaluate your self-esteem using various methods. One way is to look at your plans for the future. Where do you see yourself five years from now? Visualize what your life will be like: your work, your home, your family, and your friends. Take a minute and really try to imagine the details of your future life (refer back to the *Self-Exploration* exercise in the introduction to this book). How does your future look? Will you be safe and happy? Will you finally enjoy the good life you deserve? Can you imagine a job you enjoy, where your coworkers like and respect you? Will you be able to form an intact, secure family, free from abuse?

When you visualize yourself in the future, do you have an image of how you might look? Imagine looking at yourself in the future, completely naked, in a full-length mirror. What do you see? Do parts of your body make you feel uncomfortable or embarrassed when you imagine them? Do individual features look "ugly" to you? Are these the same parts your ex-abuser told you were ugly?

Your abuser might have focused some of his humiliating comments on your physical appearance. Many women in our culture are vulnerable to criticism about their looks. Women may be afraid they look too skinny or too fat, too short or too tall, their breasts are too small or too large. Your abuser most likely knew what would hurt the most and focused criticism on those physical characteristics.

Those beliefs may still be with you. The more criticisms of your body your abuser leveled at you, the harder it is to let go of them.

Although you now understand that the criticisms were part of the abuse, they may still affect your self-concept. You can know, intellectually, that the comments were designed to humiliate and control you. Nevertheless, dismissing them on an emotional level is difficult. It may take a long time to believe your beauty does not, by any means, depend on the judgments of a cruel, controlling, abusive partner.

Post-Traumatic Stress Disorder (Revisited)

You may be suffering to some degree from post-traumatic stress disorder (PTSD) (see Chapter 8, "When Feelings Overwhelm You"). Several emotional factors may suggest the presence of PTSD.

Do you find that the memory of the abuse (physical, sexual, emotional, etc.) suddenly, out of nowhere, consumes your thinking? A sound, sight or even an aroma, maybe a cologne or aftershave, can suddenly and without warning transport you, psychologically, right back to the abuse. This phenomenon, called *intrusive recall*, can interfere in very debilitating ways with your daily life. At times, you may feel you are having a flashback and are reliving a particularly traumatic event. At other times, you may feel as though you are having a particularly strong, almost physical, "reliving" of the abuse.

Another common symptom of PTSD is *hypervigilance*—the feeling that you must always be on your guard and can never relax. If you jump out of your skin when someone touches you from behind or at sudden loud noises, you are not completely beyond the effects of the abuse. Even a random aroma or scent can suddenly and without warning transport you, psychologically, right back to the abuse. These powerful mental and physical associations show that you still need to do some more work to get beyond the trauma you experienced.

PTSD also sometimes produces a symptom called *dissociation*, a period of disconnection between a person's sense of reality and what is actually occurring. Dissociation is the perception that you are outside your body. If your relationship was especially abusive or violent, you may have found that during an attack, you seemed to leave your physical body and were observing the beating from above, looking down on it. This ability to escape the trauma of physical abuse helped you to survive the horrors of the relationship.

All of us experience a very mild form of dissociation every now and then. A good example of this occurs when you are driving along a highway and suddenly you realize you don't remember a thing about the last five miles of your drive. At first it may scare you, but then you realize you were daydreaming, and your driving was just fine. These sorts of experiences are not caused by trauma, but may be the result of stress or distraction.

The dissociation that occurs after a traumatic event is similar to daydreams, but much more intense. Now that you are out of the abusive relationship, you may find that you dissociate in frightening ways. You may experience episodes in which you completely lose a block of time. You may have experienced periods when minutes, hours, or even days had passed, but you couldn't remember them. Survivors often have difficulty allowing their mind and body to let go of defense mechanisms they used for survival. If you are finding that you are experiencing episodes of dissociation that are interfering with your daily life, this is a clear sign that you have more healing work to do.

Avoidant Thinking

On the other hand, do you find that you push thoughts of the abuse out of your mind? Are you unable to think at all about that horrible time? Do your friends and family know the topic of the abuse is off-limits for discussion? If someone asks you about it, do you immediately turn the conversation in a different direction because it's too overwhelming to think about the abuse? Do you try anything you can think of to wipe the abuse out of your memory? Everyone prefers to not think back on painful times in their lives. If however, you are unable to think about these times without disassociating or becoming severely depressed or anxious, this is something more. These mental strategies are called *avoidant thinking* and you may engage in it because those thoughts are too painful even to allow them into your conscious mind. Until you can come to terms with the abuse, think about it, analyze it, and move past it, the pain is unlikely to go away (see Chapter 13, "Beginning to Heal"). Avoidant thinking is another sign that you are still healing.

Behavioral Signs: Connections with Others

One way to assess your healing progress is to examine your daily activities. Often, if you are not able to detect your psychological pain, you might be able to see the behavioral signs.

Now that you are out of the abusive relationship, how are your interactions with others? Have you been able to maintain some of your old friendships or establish new bonds with others? Do you feel that you have an effective support system of people you love and who love you in return?

How are your relationships with those who were there for you during and immediately after the abuse, those with whom you feel safe now? Are you able to let go of your sense of embarrassment, anger, and guilt in order to stay connected to them? Can you look them in the eyes and feel like an equal, or do you continue to feel indebted to them in a way that makes you feel small? If you do not feel strong and equal to your friends, this indicates additional healing is needed.

What about those who were not there for you during the abuse, those who abandoned you? Have you decided where or if they fit into your life now? It's all up to you. You may decide some of them should not be in your life anymore. Perhaps others are important and meaningful to you, and you feel a need to keep them in your life, despite their inability to support you during the abuse (see Chapter 11, "The Reactions of Others"). Do you feel comfortable with the roles these people have in your life now? If not, you may still be struggling with your recovery process.

Consider the new people in your life. Do you worry they will hurt you in some way? Do you feel inferior around them because you were in an abusive relationship? Whenever you sense the smallest glitch in your friendship, do you panic and go overboard trying to make it OK again? Do you fear that these new friends might not be there for you when you need them? These doubts and insecurities are perfectly normal in light of the abuse you suffered. It may be hard to trust anyone again, but you need a support network of friends and family. If your answers to the questions in this section demonstrate your ongoing distrust and fear of getting close to others, this is a sign that there is still work to be done.

Taking Care of Yourself

In the time following the abusive relationship, how well have you taken care of yourself? Are you being good to yourself or are you focusing most of your caring energy on others? If you look at your life objectively, does it seem as though you are doing more for others than you are for yourself? Do you go out of your way to assist and tend to others who are having a difficult time? What about when

you are the one having a rough time? Are you able to care for yourself as well as you care for them?

Immersing yourself in the problems of others may be a way of
hiding from yourself, of avoiding the pain and discomfort of
working through *your* trauma. If you can spend all your time thinking of others, you don't have to think about yourself. What it really
means is that you are still not ready to deal with your own pain, and
dealing with that is key to healing.

Taking Care of Your Physical Health

The mind–body connection, that is, your emotional well-being and
your physical health, are closely linked. How well are you taking
care of your body? Do you listen when your body informs you that
you are tired and run down? If you get sick, do you allow yourself
to relax and get well or do you force yourself to go on, no matter
what? Do you find it difficult to allow others to take care of you?
Think back to a time when you were ill before the abuse. Were
you this hard on yourself back then? If not, your refusal now to
give your body a break may be related to the aftereffects of the
abuse. This may be a way of denying any weakness or even punish-
ing yourself. Whatever the exact connection, it is a further sign
there is still work that you need to do to overcome the effects of the
abuse.

Dealing with nutrition and food may be a problem for you if your
abuser destroyed your body image. If you severely restrict your food
intake, diet excessively, exercise compulsively, eat in binges, or are
caught up in binge and purge cycles, you need to focus your healing
efforts on these potentially dangerous and self-abusive behaviors (see
Chapter 13, "Beginning to Heal").

If you are using alcohol or other drugs to escape from your frightening emotions and memories, you are still suffering the effects of
the abuse. If you are using more alcohol or other drugs, using
different or stronger drugs, or getting high more often than you did
before, this is an indication of the continuing presence of the abuse
in your life. Although it is a very common coping strategy, abusing
substances can delay healing and prevent you from regaining your
life. Your abuser doesn't deserve to continue to have this much
power over you. If you feel your substance use is out of your control,
many resources are available to help you overcome your addictions
and continue down the path of healing (see "Resources" at the end
of this book).

Some survivors of abusive and violent relationships engage in self-injurious behaviors. This is discussed in Chapter 8, "When Feelings Overwhelm You," but it is important enough to mention again here. Have you cut, burned, or physically hurt yourself in other ways? Many survivors experience a sense of numbness that overwhelms them even after the relationship is over. Wounding themselves is a test to see if they can feel. For others, such injuries are signs of self-loathing or self-punishment that stem from extremely low levels of self-worth.

Help with Healing

The signs of unfinished healing discussed in this chapter are just some of the most common indications that you have work left to do. Other signs are sure to exist that are unique to you and your life. The fact that you can recognize that you may not yet have recovered fully from the abuse is a healthy part of the healing process. This awareness allows you to continue to move toward becoming the person you want to be and having the fulfilling life you desire.

Keep in mind, if you find this process too difficult to do on your own, you might want to consider finding some help. As we have mentioned before, seeking help in the form of a crisis center advocate, counselor, or medical professional does not mean that you are weak or that there is something wrong with you. It means that you have the courage and strength to do what it takes to reclaim your life after an abusive relationship (see Chapter 13, "Beginning to Heal").

Assessing Your Healing

The following exercise is designed to help you find out how your healing process is going. Complete the exercise as honestly and completely as you can; no one needs to see it but you.

Rate how you see each of the following issues in your life as they are today:

Life Issue	Rating				
	Very Good	Good	Just OK	Not So Good	Does Not Apply To Me
Your overall self-esteem					
Your ability to reach your life goals					
Your personal safety					
The safety of your children					
Your work or career life					
Your level of happiness					
Your intelligence					
Your talents					
Your sense of humor					
Your ability to care for others					
Your personal attractiveness					
Your ability to make friends					
Your relationships with existing friends					
Your family					
Relationships					
Interactions with acquaintances					
Relationships with coworkers					

Life Issue	Rating				
	Very Good	Good	Just OK	Not So Good	Does Not Apply To Me
Taking time just for yourself					
Treating yourself well					
Putting your needs first					
Taking care of yourself physically					
Not getting overly tired					
Taking care of yourself when ill					
Eating well					
Sleeping well					
Exercising regularly					
Your overuse of alcohol and other drugs					

Now take a look at how you have rated the items.

- If you have rated the majority of these life issues in the "very good" or "good" columns you are already well on your way toward healing.
- If you have checks in many different columns but overall they seem to average out on the "good side," you are beginning to heal and should be able to continue to feel better about yourself and your life.
- If the majority of your ratings are "just OK" and "not so good," you may just be in the beginning stages of moving on in your life, or it may indicate that you are "stuck" and are having a difficult time moving on.

In order to track your healing process, *repeat this exercise in a month or so.* If your "scores" have not improved or are still mostly "just OK" or "not so good," this is a sign that you may be continuing to experience difficulty healing from the abuse and moving on with your life. (Please refer to Chapter 13, "Beginning to Heal" and Chapter 14, "Who Are You Now?")

10

What About the Children?

Myth: An abusive father is better than no father at all.

Myth: Abusers rarely target the children.

Myth: If children never witness the actual abuse, they are usually not traumatized by it.

*T*his chapter is for those of you who have children who experienced the nightmare of abuse, whether they were directly abused by your former partner or witnessed the abuse you endured. Sadly, many abusive relationships include children in various family configurations: biological children, children from a previous marriage, or foster children. No matter how your children were (or are) related to your former abuser, they may be suffering the consequences of the abuse. Witnessing relationship abuse and violence can have devastating effects on anyone, especially children. The majority of partner abusers also abuse their children.

Research has shown that since children's brains are still developing, those who witness or experience abuse can have changes to brain that creates emotional or even physical effects. Your children need not have been the direct recipients of abuse to suffer profound psychological and emotional effects. All children who live in homes where domestic violence occurs suffer to some degree. Witnessing a parent being victimized is terribly frightening and confusing for children. This chapter is for those of you who brought your children out of the violent relationship with you. It focuses on the aftereffects of the abusive relationship on your children, how to protect them from your abuser, and what you can do to help them recover and heal along with you.

The Children's Experience of the Abuse

First, even if you tried to hide the abuse from your kids or camouflage it, they knew about it. Your children probably lived in fear and confusion. They were afraid of being abused themselves, they were afraid for you, and they were afraid of losing the people they depended on to care for them. They may not have been able to understand who was to blame and what should happen because your abuser was always telling them everything was your fault. They were confused because their environment was unpredictable as a result of the recurring abuse around them. Above all, the children, just like you, probably felt very distressed that anyone, especially this other significant person in their lives (whom they felt they loved, regardless of anything he may have done), could treat you in such a way. They probably began to question their own judgment about people and relationships.

Safety and consistency are two necessary conditions for children to grow up emotionally healthy. Despite your best efforts, you may not have been able to provide these circumstances for your children. While your children were enduring the abusive relationship, they had neither safety nor consistency. Your children found themselves in a situation where they could never be sure from one day to the next if they had a parent who would be able to be there for them. They questioned if they could trust the abuser, and, often, you were so physically and emotionally traumatized, they were reluctant to ask you for what few resources you had left. If they did ask, you may not have been in any condition to give them what they needed at the time. And just as you never felt safe, your children probably didn't either.

This was not your fault. You had little control over your life then. Throughout this book, we often discuss your need to do whatever was necessary to survive. Chances are you were also doing what was necessary to ensure the survival of your children. Survival took priority over perfect parenting. Remember, you got your kids out of a dangerous situation: *You rescued them.* As you discover your path toward healing, you will realize this and usually find that your children will recover as you do.

Although reactions of children who witness relationship abuse and domestic violence vary from child to child, some categories of responses are fairly typical. If the children were themselves abused, the effect on them may be even more pronounced. Your ability to recognize in your children the psychological, emotional, and behavioral effects of the abuse will assist you in guiding them through their healing process.

Psychological and Emotional Reactions

Children's psychological and emotional reactions to abusive relationships will vary depending on the nature of the abuse, their overall adjustment prior to the abuse, and their individual personality characteristics. However, just like with you, witnessing abuse or experiencing it firsthand can make them more vulnerable to PTSD. Given that their brains ae still developing they are even more likely to develop problems associated with the abuse. Because the symptoms discussed here occur more frequently in children who witness abuse or are victims themselves, keeping a close eye on your children will help you detect whether some of these signs are present.

Your children may exhibit *physical* and *psychological problems*. For instance, children of abused parents sometimes show delays in thinking, verbal, and motor skills development. They experience sleep disorders (which may or may not be associated with depression), and psychosomatic illnesses (illnesses that are real, but that have no physical cause, such as frequent stomachaches or headaches). In addition, they tend to be more impulsive than average, engaging in inappropriate behaviors without regard for potential negative consequences.

Your children may experience many of the same strong emotions you felt during and in the aftermath of your abusive relationship. Probably the most common, and entirely normal, emotional responses in children are *anxiety* and *depression*. Your children may, to an even greater extent than yourself, perceive the abuse to have been completely beyond their control.

Even if you are in a situation now where you know your children are out of danger, *they* may not understand that they are safe. They may be too young to comprehend all of the precautions you have taken to ensure their safety. They observed that you were unable to protect yourself, and possibly them, from the violence in the past, so they may continue to feel afraid not only for themselves but also for you. They know they were unable to stop the abuse in the past, so they feel they would be powerless to prevent or stop it now. How could such a looming threat *not* produce severe anxiety?

Although you have reduced or eliminated contact with your abuser, the children may still be in contact through court-ordered visitation or joint custody (this is discussed in greater detail in Chapter 12, "Practical Considerations"). Although safeguards may be in place to prevent any further obvious abuse during the children's visits with your abuser, understand that feeling safe may be difficult for them. It is possible that your children may feel even greater anxiety than you do.

Low self-esteem is perhaps the most common characteristic to watch for in your children. This is one of the most pervasive and debilitating of all the psychological effects. As we discussed earlier, your children may feel at fault for the abuse and guilty for being unable to stop it. They may view themselves as failures. This poor self-image has the potential to affect negatively nearly everything they attempt in school, sports, personal goals, and relationships with others.

Your children's perception of powerlessness over bad events in their lives may lead to *depression*. The symptoms of depression in children are similar to those in adults. They include social withdrawal, frequent and easily provoked crying, a lack of enthusiasm for fun activities, lack of energy, changes in sleeping and eating habits, and, sometimes, suicidal thoughts.

Self-blame is another strong emotion your children may express following the abusive relationship. Your kids love their parents unconditionally; they may even express love for your abuser despite the abuse or violence. They desperately want their parents to be happy, to get along, not to hurt each other, and to love them back. They may believe that if they had behaved differently or somehow "better" you would all be happy and together.

Usually, related to this self-blame, is intense *guilt*. If you have older children, they might feel they should have done something to intervene, to stop the abuse, to prevent you from being hurt. When older children try to step in, the results can be catastrophic. The child can be seriously injured or killed, or, in some cases, the child may seriously injure or kill the abuser. Many children, however, are too afraid, and feel far too helpless to attempt to intervene. They have no choice but to live in silence with the fear and terror of the abuse. If your children tried to intervene, they risked serious emotional and physical consequences for them and for you. If they tried, but were unable to help, their guilt may be intense.

From a relatively safe vantage point in the aftermath of the abuse, another emotion often emerges in children, as it may have in you: *anger*. As your children witnessed the abuse and violence, it was probably very clear that expressions of anger on their part were out of the question. They knew it would be dangerous and might make the abuse worse or turn it against them. Now that you and they are out, the anger can awaken. It might be expressed as rage toward the abuser, outrage toward you for, in the child's mind, "allowing" the abuse to happen, or blaming you for breaking up the family. Children may engage in abusive acts toward you, their siblings, or their peers, modeled after the behaviors they witnessed in your abuser. They may also experience hostility toward themselves for believing they somehow caused or failed to prevent the abuse.

Finally, your children may suffer *fear of abandonment*. During the abusive relationship, they may have felt helpless and terrified that their parents would not be there for them. Although their safety now depends upon being away from your abuser, they may feel abandoned by him nonetheless.

Many uncontrollable and horrible events have occurred in your children's lives. How can they be sure the one parent they have, you, won't go away too? Eventually, over time, they will regain the trust and faith that you will be there for them, but fearing abandonment now, and perhaps for a while, is normal, and from their perspective, justified.

Behavioral Difficulties

If your children are unable to work out their psychological problems verbally, you might find they engage in difficult behaviors. These behaviors depend on the age of the child but may include tantrums, greater-than-normal sibling aggression, running away from home, self-injurious behavior (head banging, cutting, burning, etc.), violent behavior toward pets or other animals, drug and alcohol abuse, and sexual impulsivity. Children act out on occasion when angry or frustrated, but the behaviors mentioned here tend to be more common in children who have witnessed or experienced domestic abuse.

It would be a relief to know that any effects of the abuse would be evident immediately, so you can find ways to support your children. Unfortunately, exposure to domestic violence may influence adjustment and behavior later in the child's life. The safety, reassurance, and help you give your children now will significantly reduce their risk for difficulties later.

Making It Better

Being a good parent is never easy and no one is the "perfect" parent. Parenting may be even more difficult now, as you are dealing with your own often painful and stressful healing process. Your kids are the most important priority in your life, so you experience even more guilt and more stress when you feel unable to give them the time and energy they need from you. Some survivors find at times that they displace the anger they feel toward their abuser onto their children. You may have found yourself becoming angry more quickly with your children, lashing out verbally more often when they misbehave, or even resorting to physical punishment you later regretted. After what you've been through, and considering the energy you need to expend on reclaiming *your* life, finding your emotions on a short fuse at times is understandable—the same is true for your kids. If you are seeing negative changes in your relationship with your children, it's important to pay close attention to how and when your frustration with them builds toward an unwanted outburst.

If your children are required to spend time with your ex-partner, they may find this experience confusing, uncomfortable, and even frightening. They may express these feelings before or after their visits as hostility toward you in the form of misbehavior, ignoring you, or verbal displays of anger directed at you. Upon their return you may also see the results of your ex attempting to use the children against you. (See Chapter 16, "Is Your Abuser Still in Your Life?" for more on this issue.)

What can you do to help your children heal? Above all, try not to take their acting out personally. It's not easy, but remember, they may be directing some of these emotions toward you because you are their only safe outlet. This makes it even more important that you have a support system of your own with whom you can discuss these issues.

If your children are old enough to understand, explain to them that this is a difficult time, and everyone is on edge. Tell them that it's OK that you are all a little more touchy than usual. Let them know that eventually this will pass. Make sure that they know that you love them no matter what.

If you have more than one child, try to schedule one-on-one time with each of them. Often what one child needs to hear, say, or discuss is very different from what the other children need. Allow them to express their thoughts and feelings in their own way. There is no right or wrong way for them to react. Encourage them to talk about the abuse and about your abuser.

As difficult as it may be, try to explain to them what happened without becoming angry or defensive yourself. Help them to identify what it is they are feeling, and let them know that it's OK to feel that way. Often children may have difficulty identifying what they are feeling, and by acknowledging it and naming it (fear, anger, guilt) you are helping them to understand themselves better. Make sure they know they can always come to you to talk about anything (see "Talking to the Children" later in this chapter for more detail).

Talk to your children about relationship violence. Avoid verbally attacking your abuser, because your children may still feel love for him. But discuss with them how no one should ever hurt anyone. Explain what this means and the effects of violence and abuse. They need to know not only that no one should ever abuse another but also that no one deserves to be abused.

Allow them the time they need to heal. Because the abuse probably occurred during some critical developmental stages, you may find that some of their emotions or behaviors are a bit "younger" than those of other kids their age. This is natural given the circumstances. Remember they also experienced the fear that you may still feel. Do whatever helps to soothe their fears. Allow them to sleep with a night light on or their door open. If they are truly fearful for their safety or yours, you may want to consider putting a baby monitor in each of their rooms. Let them know you are there for them.

Give your children some extra loving. Increase the number of hugs and pats on the back if it feels safe and comfortable to them. Spend a few extra minutes with them at bedtime. Try to offer some extra fun together in a setting in which everyone feels good. This could be anything from going to the park for a picnic to watching a movie at home. Remind them of all their good qualities more frequently. These little gestures can go a long way toward reversing the effects of the strong negative emotions everyone is experiencing during this difficult time.

Develop some strategies to defuse emotional situations before they get out of control. These could include each family member designating a code word or sentence that signals they need a two-minute truce during which no one may speak (so *everyone* has the power to stop the escalation process). Trying to get all family members to talk about how they are feeling (using "I" statements) rather than what someone else said or did ("He said that..." "She just...") may help to keep arguments from becoming as severe. Or you may want to have regular family meetings in which everyone is free to discuss anything without fear of punishment or ridicule. These are just a few suggestions. You can develop your own interventions, maybe in consultation with your kids if they are old enough, or with a therapist, if you have one, who is working with the children or with you.

Finally, find some time for yourself away from your children. This should be quality time, not when you are at work or when they are visiting your abuser and you are worrying about them. If possible, try to set up a few hours each week when your kids can visit a friend's house or go to a trusted relative of yours. This will help prevent the frustrations among you from building up to explosive levels.

Keep in mind, these strategies will probably not work every time. There are bound to be flare-ups, tantrums, and eruptions from time to time. But by thinking about what causes them and how to prevent or defuse them and by planning ahead, the number and intensity can usually be minimized. If nothing helps, and your relationship with your kids continues to be difficult, some professional family counseling might be in order (this is further discussed later in this chapter).

Keeping Your Children Safe

All of the safety information discussed in Chapter 2, "Are You Out of Danger Now?" pertains to the safety of your children as well. Beyond those important safeguards, the key to keeping your children safe is to prevent your abuser from having access to them.

If your abuser has no legal access, be alert to illegal attempts to see the children. The motives for this may be feelings of love and a desire to see the children. More often, however, your former abuser will try to use the children to control and frighten *you*.

If you believe that your former partner may try to contact your children, you need to enlist the assistance and cooperation of everyone with whom the children spend time. All caretakers must be made aware of the possible danger. As discussed in Chapter 2, you should supply childcare locations, schools, organized sports or other activity leaders, and babysitters with information, descriptions, and photos of your abuser and instruct them *exactly* to whom the child may be released. Today, most agencies with responsibilities for children are aware of these issues, but you should always double-check.

If your children are old enough to be without supervision at times, be sure they understand the reasons it would be unwise and possibly not safe for them to allow your former abuser to contact or talk to them. You can tell them that due to the possible danger they are not to go anywhere with your abuser that has not been clearly approved by you. Explain to your children that though they may love and enjoy the time they spend with your ex-partner, it's important to stick to planned visits so the good times never again have to become bad times.

Explain to your older children what they should do if your abuser approaches them. Review your safety plan with them so they will know how to get out of the house in an emergency. Be sure they know that if your ex shows up uninvited, they should leave immediately and not stay and talk. Have safe houses of friends and relatives and other locations such as stores or offices, and "safe people" identified where they can go if your abuser approaches them when you are not around. Your children should understand that they don't need to spend every minute being afraid, but they must grasp the potential consequences of interacting with your ex and be prepared to act.

Custody and Visitation Rights

Many abusive partners may choose to fight in court for custody of the children following the breakup of a violent relationship. Not only is custody an opportunity for an abuser to exercise control, but it may also be perceived as an opportunity to prove that the accusations of abuse are unfounded. Remember, most abusers are experts at hiding their violent nature and can appear very loving and even victimized. Even worse, your abuser may use your children as a vehicle for continued abuse of you by questioning them about your activities, blaming you for breaking up the family, and attempting to convince the children that you don't love them.

If you believe the visitation rights granted by the court place them or you in greater danger, your best course of action is to continue to fight the decision legally. This can be expensive, but many organizations and legal clinics provide this form of assistance for little or no fee (see Chapter 12, "Practical Considerations").

Talking to the Children

In deciding how to explain to the children the pain, abuse, and emotional trauma they have seen, you should rely on your own judgment and intuition to decide what they need and want to hear relative to their ages. However, some basic principles can be incorporated into all discussions.

1. Your children have a right to and a need for truthful, age-appropriate information about what they witnessed and why the abuser is not living with them anymore. Younger children will usually accept an explanation about how mad your ex became sometimes and how it was better if they lived apart. Older children can usually understand and handle the concept of your abuser's tendencies to be jealous, controlling, or violent, and why it was necessary to separate. As we discussed earlier, children need to be told, as accurately as possible, what threat, if any, your abuser poses to them now.
2. Your children, especially the younger ones, may still love your abuser, although they have seen or experienced terrible events. They need to be allowed to have these feelings, but know that they cannot be together right now.

3. Telling the children that your abuser is a "bad" person will probably only further upset and confuse them and will not be helpful in the long run. Instead, talk to them about the abusive *behaviors* (yelling, threatening, hitting) and how they were difficult, dangerous, or scary, rather than making sweeping statements about your ex's overall character.

4. Children need to be told firmly and frequently that you are doing everything you can to keep them safe (refer to Chapter 2, "Are You Out of Danger Now?") and you will always be there for them. Obviously, there are no absolute guarantees in life, but this is a fundamental message all children need in their lives, regardless of the abuse.

5. Children need to feel they are loved unconditionally by you. You can help them to feel this by telling them so, often and directly. Try to take the time to look into the child's eyes, touch or hold the child, and say, "I love you." This goes much farther than a quick perfunctory "Love you," as you say goodnight and turn off the light. Also, when disciplining them, be sure to let them know that you are displeased with their behavior, not with them as people. Say, "I'm very upset that you did that," not "You are so stupid to have done that."

6. Children need to be reassured in every possible way that the abuse and the breakup of the relationship were not their fault. Try not to wait for them to bring this up, but instead talk to each child individually to explain that the problem was with your abuser. Tell each child in a way he or she can understand that the children did nothing wrong and that they are not to blame for the breakup.

7. Children should be told clearly that all forms of abuse and violence are wrong. This is often difficult to understand fully in a culture that often glorifies violence. When they are old enough to understand, talk to them about how media violence is related to the violence they have experienced personally in their lives. Let them know that they can play an effective role in reducing and preventing violence not just in their own lives but in society in general.

8. Children should learn from their mother that they have a right to be loved and not harmed and must never accept abusive behavior. It is probably better not to try to hide or deny what happened, but instead to discuss it as openly as is age-appropriate, and use personal experience as an example of unacceptable behavior in any relationship.

Children need to be told, in all possible ways, that the abuse they saw or experienced in your relationship was wrong, it should never happen to anyone, and it has no place in a loving relationship.

Should You Seek Professional Help for Your Children?

If you have a child who appears to be extremely affected by the abuse, specially trained therapists can help the child deal with the trauma of domestic violence. Some general guidelines can assist you in estimating your children's need for outside help (these guidelines appear in greater detail in the *Self-Exploration* exercise at the end of this chapter). Consider the various emotional, psychological, and behavioral symptoms discussed earlier. Note any of the symptoms you see in your child. Then consider each of the observed signs on the following three dimensions.

The first dimension is *frequency*: How often does your child display a particular symptom? Generally, the more often a symptom appears, the greater the need for some kind of treatment. Next is *intensity*: How strong is the symptom when it appears? If the emotion, the psychological difficulty, or the behavior is especially intense, that is, clearly identifiable and impossible to ignore, a greater need for professional intervention may be indicated. Finally, you will need to consider the dimension of *interference with functioning*: To what extent are the symptoms interfering with your child's daily life in school, at home, with friends, and his or her relationship with you? If several symptoms rate high on these dimensions, an appointment with a professional counselor might be a very good idea.

How to Find Help for Your Children

There are several ways to locate counselors who are specifically trained to deal with post-abuse problems. If you are not sure which therapists in your area have this specialized training, check with your local domestic violence crisis center or abuse hotline for recommendations and referrals. Many counselors provide services on a sliding price scale, meaning that the fees they charge will be reduced for those clients with lower incomes.

If you continue to have difficulty finding a qualified professional to assist your children, call the National Domestic Violence Hotline at 1-800-799-SAFE or see its Web site at www.thehotline.org. This Web site will direct you to local domestic violence crisis centers that can help you find help. In addition to crisis intervention information, the hotline also maintains an extensive list of counseling resources by city and state and should be able to provide referrals in your area.

If you think one or more of your children may need some profes- sional assistance, but you are not sure, one way to find out is to schedule a preliminary visit with a family violence or abuse coun- selor for evaluation and assessment. If the therapist concludes that the child is doing well and does not need further intervention, you will feel a weight has been lifted from your shoulders. On the other hand, if the outcome of the assessment suggests counseling is needed, you will then be clear about needing to provide it. (Refer to Chapter 13, "Beginning to Heal," for additional information on obtaining counseling.)

Your children are going through this healing process with you. As you feel stronger and more able to cope with life, you model these successes for your children.

Child Assessment

Below is a list of emotional, psychological, and behavioral difficulties children sometimes experience in the aftermath of an abusive relationship. Using your own best judgment, rate each item on the list in *all three dimensions* using the following scales for each of your children.

RATING SCALES

Almost Never   Very Often

| 1 | 2 | 3 | 4 | 5 | 6 | 7 | 8 | 9 | 10 |

Frequency of Symptom

Extremely Mild   Extremely Intense

| 1 | 2 | 3 | 4 | 5 | 6 | 7 | 8 | 9 | 10 |

Intensity of Symptom

Almost None   Nearly Constant

| 1 | 2 | 3 | 4 | 5 | 6 | 7 | 8 | 9 | 10 |

Interference with Desired Functioning

Rate the Following Behaviors Using the Rating Scales Above

Symptom	Frequency 1–10	Intensity 1–10	Interference 1–10
Suicidal thoughts**	___	___	___
Alcohol abuse**	___	___	___
Other drug abuse**	___	___	___
Animal cruelty**	___	___	___
Self-injury**	___	___	___
Anxiety	___	___	___
Social withdrawal	___	___	___
Crying	___	___	___

Copyright material from Meg Kennedy Dugan and Roger R. Hock (2018), *It's My Life Now*, Routledge

Rate the Following Behaviors Using the Rating Scales Above

Symptom	Frequency 1–10	Intensity 1–10	Interference 1–10
Not having fun	___	___	___
Sleep problems	___	___	___
Eating problems	___	___	___
Self-blame	___	___	___
Guilt	___	___	___
Fear of abandonment	___	___	___
Low self-esteem	___	___	___
Delays in motor skills	___	___	___
Verbal language delays	___	___	___
Psychosomatic illness	___	___	___
Poor impulse control	___	___	___
Tantrums	___	___	___
Fighting with siblings	___	___	___
Destroying property	___	___	___
Throwing objects	___	___	___

Note 1: The first five items marked ** are of especially great concern. If your child is experiencing any of these, *regardless of the degree*, you need to consider immediate professional support.

Note 2: If your child scores low on this scale, but you feel he or she needs some professional assistance, follow your instincts. No single scale can measure such a need with 100 percent accuracy and no one knows your child better than you.

When you have finished, analyze your ratings for all the symptoms on all three dimensions. Use the following guidelines for interpreting your ratings and making decisions about your child's need for counseling.

- Ratings of 1 or 2 on any single item in any of the columns indicate that there may be little need for concern (except for the items marked **).

- A rating of 3 or 4 on any single item in any column indicates a need to be mildly concerned about these behaviors. Counseling may not be needed at this time, but it would be a good idea to be alert to these behaviors in the future.
- A rating of 5 or 6 on any single item in any column indicates a need for moderate concern about these behaviors. Counseling might be helpful now in dealing with them and preventing them from becoming worse.
- Scores of 7 or higher on any single item in any column indicate a serious problem may exist. Your child would benefit greatly by receiving counseling now or in the very near future.

11

The Reactions of Others

Myth: Your true friends will understand and accept what happened in your relationship.

Myth: It's better to have family and friends around you, even if they don't understand, than to be alone.

Myth: You can count on your friends and family to deal with the aftermath of the abuse and support you unconditionally.

As you rebuild your new life you will need to decide who will be part of it and who won't. These decisions are completely up to you, and they can be among the most difficult you have to make. Making your best decisions about keeping people in your life will take time and careful introspection. The only sure thing is that you *need* others in your life to support you, to be friends with you, and to love you.

Ask yourself the following three questions when trying to decide whether someone is to be a part of your life now and in the future:

1. Is this person someone who can support and love me?
2. Does this person create positive feelings about who I am and the choices I have made in freeing myself from an abusive relationship?
3. Do I feel I can trust this person completely?

If you can answer these questions in the affirmative, your decision should be easier. However, the answers may be more difficult than they seem. Your responses may depend on several important factors about the person and about you.

People Who Failed to Support You in the Past

All of us experience difficult times in our lives. Most of us believe our family and friends will always be there for us. We expect they will love and support us no matter what. When this doesn't happen, we can feel devastated. The anger, disappointment, and loss we experience in those situations can make any future intimate bond with them seem impossible.

People who were not there for you during your abusive relationship might be the most difficult to keep in your life. They may include your family members, his family members, your friends, or your coworkers. A variety of reasons may exist for why they let you down, perhaps due to their inability to accept the reality of the abuse or due to the forced isolation your abuser created. They may have felt abandoned by *you*.

You may discover you do not want those who you feel abandoned you during the abusive relationship back in your life. If you believe you cannot move past your negative feelings toward them, eventually you may need to cut ties with them. In some cases, however, you may decide you need time to heal from your "wounds" and then reevaluate your relationship with them.

If you decide you would like some of these people to reenter your life, you will need to find ways to communicate with them about what happened. If you continue to harbor adverse feelings toward them and cannot openly deal with them, those feelings are sure to surface in unproductive ways. Try talking to them about your feelings and about their lack of support in the past. See if you can come to an understanding that truly allows your differences to be set aside. If you can accomplish this, you may have created a strong friendship and support that might last for the rest of your life.

Those Who Denied the Abuse

It may help to understand why some people failed to support you. One reason may be they didn't believe the abuse was happening or wouldn't accept how bad it was. If this rings true, think about why they doubted you. If they are related to your former partner, they were probably blind to any flaws in him. Abusers are very talented at hiding their controlling and abusive sides from others, including family members; others were probably convinced that such horrible behaviors were simply impossible.

Other people may have tried to justify your abuser's actions with the excuse that your abuser endured a difficult or even abusive childhood and doesn't really know how to express feelings of love. They may have gone to great lengths to explain to you all of the difficulties your former abuser experienced in the past and how he had worked so hard to overcome them. They may have told you how good you were for him and how much he needed you. They had a way of making *you* feel guilty for condemning him for the abuse.

These people are unlikely to see your experience any differently now. In fact, he has probably convinced them you were at fault for the failure of the relationship. Unless something very convincing has altered their beliefs, their judgments of you and the relationship may never change. You need to decide if keeping such people in your life offers you anything of value.

Those Who Blamed You

Some people may not only have failed to support you, but actually blamed you. When you told these people about an abusive incident they immediately asked something like, "What did you do to cause such an outburst?" Or, "Obviously, you should not have done that!" They gave you advice about how relationships are difficult and how you needed to stick it out and try harder. Some of them may have even told you the abuse was due to your behavior and you are the one who must change to remedy the problem.

It's important for you to look at the reasons these people behaved this way. Try not to obsess about the past, but try to determine how they are likely to act in the future. You may need to decide if you feel you can forgive them (and this may not be possible for you), and assess whether or not a future relationship with them is in your best interests (see "Do You Need to Forgive?" later in this chapter).

Those who have an ingrained belief that men can do whatever they want in a love relationship are probably not people you want in your life. They will remind you forever that you made a mistake, in their eyes, when you left your abuser. They may judge your future relationships and interfere with your need to make the choices that are best for you.

You may feel uncomfortable breaking off unwanted relationships because they are family members or old friends, or because you fear hurting their feelings. But no one should ever feel obligated to be friends with those who do not enrich their life. If your instincts tell you they will not ever be able to accept the truth of what happened and will be unable to support your decisions, follow those instincts to distance yourself from them.

One way to look at it is that you endured so much pain, and it took such strength and courage to get out of that abusive relationship, all of your new relationships should be on *your* terms. This is not selfish or egotistical. It is taking care of *you*. Recognize the qualities you need from your close friend and family relationships and ensure they are present in the connections you decide to maintain. Feel free to set boundaries for what treatment you will not accept from others.

Those Who Did Not Know How to Help

Many of your friends and family members may fall into this category. They love you and they wanted to help you in your time of need. Nevertheless, they simply did not know what to say or do. Their intentions were good, but they were unable to improve your situation.

A common example of this involves family and friends who were always urging you to leave. They could not understand why that was so difficult and complex an issue for you. Perhaps, as time went on and you were still in the relationship, they began to be less sympathetic about the abuse. Even if they didn't say so, it seemed to you that they were thinking, "I told you so." Eventually, their opinions made you feel increasingly at fault and less and less comfortable confiding in them.

Now that you have left that relationship, reestablishing relationships with these friends and relatives may be difficult. They may go to great lengths to remind you how awful your relationship was and throw in comments such as, "I'll never understand why you stayed so long," or "I would never have put up with that." You may see these people as your friends, but find yourself frequently defensive and uncomfortable around them. Explaining to them over and over that getting out wasn't easy at all and was much more complicated than they could ever imagine, is wearing you out.

If you are trying to decide whether to keep these people in your life, you have to examine the emotional impact they have on you now. Some of these friends may give you support, respect, and friendship despite their past "shortcomings." With some of them, you may be able to tune out their shortsightedness and cherish the good parts of your relationship. Others may start to understand better what you went through and begin to offer you support.

On the other hand, if you find their judgmental view of the abusive relationship negates the positives, you may want to reexamine the value of their friendship. You can try talking with these friends and explain to them how their attitudes affect you: Tell them that when they judge your actions you feel guilty, sad, and angry. If they seem to get it, you can try making them allies in your healing process. Explain that you realize abusive relationships can be difficult to understand, but now that you are out, you need to move on and avoid dwelling on the past. Although they weren't there for you then, they may be able to be here for you now.

Those Who Knew, but Did Nothing

What about the people who knew about the abuse, but chose to ignore it? The knowledge of what was happening to you may have been too painful for them to accept. They may have felt they didn't know what to say or do, and, therefore, did nothing. Unfortunately, many friends and family members of abuse survivors, when questioned later, say they didn't want to intrude or they didn't want to risk losing the friendship (yours or his) by interfering.

Perhaps their silent acceptance of the abuse now feels like a betrayal. It's easy once you are out to think that if only someone had been there for you, that terrible time in your life would have been different. But is that really true? Assessing your relationships with these "silent" friends involves evaluating whether their intervention in the abuse would have changed anything. Could they have said or done anything to stop the abuse? See if you can talk with these friends about their silence. Don't confront or accuse them, but just ask them why they didn't talk about it with you. You may be surprised by their answers.

Some might insist they did acknowledge the abuse. They might assert they remember being empathetic often, but they always got the feeling *you* didn't want to discuss it. Abuse is a very difficult subject to bring up with someone you love. You may fear alienating or angering that person. Some of your friends may have feared losing you if they were to push the subject. They may say they were there for you, but left it up to you to initiate discussions about the abuse. They may have seen your relationship as "personal" and felt they had no business intruding.

If you decide to mend these relationships, being honest will be important. You can talk about how you appreciate their willingness to talk now and focus on whatever support they gave you. You may want to tell them you understand how terribly difficult it was for them to say anything. Listening to their version of past events, without becoming defensive, can be helpful. They may have given you subtle signs of concern, but you were in no condition at the time to pick up on them at the time. If you can relieve the tension and open up to each other, these may be among your future friends.

Those Who "Told You" What to Do

You may have had some friends and family members who believed they were going to be the ones to "rescue you." They probably felt they were your only "real" supporters because they told you exactly what you should and should not do to fix the problem. They were exceedingly free with their advice and always seemed to know what was best for you.

These people probably had your welfare at heart. They believed if you "didn't know what was good for you," they would help you understand. They felt they knew what was wrong or right and they could guide you in the best direction. Unfortunately, without realizing it, they may have been just what you did *not* need: more people trying to control your life.

Now that you are out of the abusive relationship and in charge of your own life, your contacts with this group of people may feel strained. They may still want to control you. You probably feel their attempts at control when you hear them say things such as, "You're not going to allow the children to see your ex, are you?" or "It's too soon for you to date again. What will people think?" These judgmental comments may undermine your confidence to make decisions that are best for you and to take charge of your life.

Nearly everyone at times may get a bit too "pushy" with a friend they believe is in trouble or in pain. All of us may try to guide that person we care about to a better situation. It often makes sense for people who are having a difficult time to take into consideration the insights and opinions of those they trust. These people, however, after offering their wisdom and advice, should then be able and willing to step back and allow you to guide your own life. If they can do that, they may be able to become a positive part of your support system. If they can't, it may be a warning sign of their controlling nature; and you don't need that in your life right now.

Do You Need to Forgive?

Did you grow up hearing it is always better to forgive and forget? Were you raised to believe that happiness requires acceptance of others' faults? Have you always believed it's necessary to forgive so that you can "move on?" The truth is, you do not *owe* anyone your forgiveness. Moreover, forgiveness is not always necessary for healing. You alone can decide who *deserves* your forgiveness. Forgiveness is a very complicated issue. The decision to forgive others rests on three conditions:

- Whether or not you believe what they did (or didn't do) were *forgivable* acts.
- Whether or not, despite their past actions, you feel it would help you to heal if you were to forgive them.
- Whether or not you feel ready to forgive.

A "right" time for forgiveness or any absolute rule about whom you must forgive do not exist. Some people forgive easily. Others hold onto resentments and anger for a long time. Much of this may be

attributed to differences in upbringing and experiences with forgiveness. Forgiving those who let you down may require time while you
heal those wounds. You may need to move beyond the fear, anger,
distrust, and sadness before you can think about forgiving. When
you truly forgive someone, it must come from your heart and you
must want to forgive. Again you are not required ever to forgive if
it's not helpful to you in your healing process. Forgiveness is a choice
and it's completely up to you.

Those Who Understood and Supported You

Having difficulties with those who really were there for you during
the abuse doesn't seem to make much sense, does it? After all, these
are the people who understood what you were going through and
stayed with you throughout. They didn't try to control your
decision-making or to judge you. They simply let you know they
cared and they would always be there for you no matter what. These
individuals are likely to continue to be your closest friends and relatives now. However, the transition to a post-abusive relationship is
not always as smooth as you might expect.

Maybe you "disappeared" during your relationship and lost
contact with these people because your abuser would not allow you
to have friends of your own. This is very common in unhealthy, controlling relationships. Maybe your abuser refused to allow you even
to see your family and friends. Maybe you didn't want to burden
them with your problems and you couldn't bear for them to know
how much you hurt. Or maybe you were afraid they would try to
come to your rescue and make things worse by forcing you to take
steps that you were not ready to take.

Even if you did not vanish from their lives, you may have been
only partially or selectively truthful with them. You probably
remember times when they asked you about why you couldn't go
somewhere with them, why you had to call home so often when you
were out, or how you got that bruise on your arm or cheek. Now
you may feel that you were not a worthy friend because you had to
lie to them so often.

Now that you are finally out of that abusive relationship, you
might find yourself feeling guilty and embarrassed around these
friends. You need to remind yourself, although you wish you had
not put them through all of that, you had no other choice at the
time. If you had confided in them completely and were "caught," the
abuse might have become much worse, and you might not have been

able to see or talk to them at all. Perhaps you also needed to convince yourself it wasn't really all that bad, so you softened your experience when you talked to them.

Whatever the reason, you now need to move beyond the guilt. You deserve all the benefits of their friendship and your friends deserve to have yours. In those close, emotionally intimate friendships, guilt and embarrassment should not play a major role. You did the best you could and they know that.

Perhaps you were able to confide in and trust some friends or relatives. They were the ones you "ran" to when things got too bad. They comforted you, listened to you, and empathized with you, over and over again. Then, each time, you'd go back to your abuser you could see the disbelief and sadness in their eyes. They may have told you how afraid they were for you and how much they worried about you. Looking back, you are amazed that anyone could have put up with you for so long. When you look at it now, it seems like a miracle that they remained so loyal and understanding.

It is never too late to thank all these people for how much their support meant and means to you. You don't need to give them gifts or find the "perfect" words. Just say what is in your heart. If saying these things directly to them is difficult for you, send them a card, a note, or even an email expressing your gratitude. Let them know that even the "little" things, the small gestures, their words of encouragement, were of enormous help to you in your time of need.

Finding New Friends and Support

Now that you are out of your abusive relationship, the characteristics you seek in new friendships might be a bit different. You might be a little (or a lot) less trusting and, therefore, you now need more time to decide how close to allow people to get to you. There is nothing wrong with being cautious in new friendships. Also, there is nothing wrong with making careful, conscious choices about whom you allow into your life.

New people in your life may not know exactly what it is you need or want from them. It will be up to you to explain to them what you need from their friendship. This may mean telling them if, when, and how to ask about your past, how to talk to you about your current life, and about the qualities you want in a friendship (such as trust, dependability, honesty, and kindness).

If you are still experiencing profound emotions related to the abuse, letting others into your life who may not understand can be difficult (see Chapter 8, "When Feelings Overwhelm You"). Again, it's smart to be cautious in new friendships, but, at the same time, building new networks of supportive friends is important. Good people exist who can truly be there for you. You need to make sure you don't build walls preventing anyone new from coming in. If you are careful, yet open, to friendships you can trust, both you, and they, win.

Evaluating Your Friendships

As you have seen throughout this book, evaluating issues in your life is sometimes easier if you write them down. This is true even when reviewing your relationships with others. No absolute method for "rating" your relationships exists ("Gee, Joey must be a better friend than Heather. He rated a 92 and Heather was only a 78!"). However, a general "analysis" to determine if you are receiving what you need from them is possible. The following exercise will help you do this. For each relationship you are questioning, complete the following form.

Person's Name or Initials _____

Characteristic or Feature	*All the Time*	*Some of the Time*	*Never*
Wants to be in my life now	_____	_____	_____
Is supportive of me now	_____	_____	_____
Made a real effort to be there for me during the abuse	_____	_____	_____
Is honest	_____	_____	_____
Is reliable	_____	_____	_____
Is trustworthy	_____	_____	_____
Values me as a person	_____	_____	_____
Is there for me even when I'm having a difficult time	_____	_____	_____
Recognizes the seriousness of what I've been through	_____	_____	_____
Can empathize with my experiences	_____	_____	_____
Wants to help but not control me	_____	_____	_____
Is nonjudgmental of me	_____	_____	_____
Has my best interests at heart	_____	_____	_____
Other(s) _____	_____	_____	_____
_____	_____	_____	_____

Now review your answers. How does this friend or family member measure up? Do your ratings agree with your intuitive feelings about this person? Use this form to begin to evaluate each of the relationships you are questioning. You can also use it to help you form an objective view of new acquaintances who may be possible future friends.

Looking Forward

12
Practical Considerations

Myth: Once you are free from the abuse, the rest of your life will be smooth and easy.

Myth: It's such a relief to be away from your abuser that daily life seems easy.

Myth: In general, survivors of domestic violence are victims who just can't make it on their own.

One of the reasons some survivors return to their abusers is that the everyday demands of life can feel overwhelming. If you are like most survivors of abuse, you know your former partner not only sought to control you but also made sure you were powerless in nearly all aspects of the relationship.

Many victims in abusive relationships find themselves cut off from the outside world. Your abuser's demands may have limited you to specific activities, and deviating from those "permitted" behaviors was not worth the risk of an abusive episode. Your shrinking self-esteem and self-confidence may have made you feel insecure and timid when you were out in the community.

The effects of losing your independence and not engaging in familiar daily activities may have surfaced when you finally left your abuser. If you are experiencing thoughts such as, "Oh, my God! How do I put my life in order all by myself?" you know the feeling. You are building a new life. This is an emotional healing process, but it also entails countless practical challenges. Unfortunately, it is these seemingly insurmountable practicalities that drive some survivors back to their former partners and continued, escalating abuse.

This chapter is devoted to discussing some of these basic life issues and to offering you some guidelines and reassurance that you *can* handle them and become a self-sufficient person.

Domestic Violence Shelters

Some survivors find that to remain safe, they need to "disappear." After escaping the relationship they may fear that if their abuser finds them, the risk of being hurt or even killed is all too real. Finding a way to "vanish" often involves finding agencies or programs that can help you.

As mentioned in Chapter 2 ("Are You Out of Danger Now?"), your local crisis center shelters should be able to provide you with protected housing on a short-term basis. Maximum lengths of stay vary from shelter to shelter. The staff at the shelters can also assist you in finding ways to stay safe after leaving the security of the shelter.

Many states now have programs called *Address Confidentiality Programs*. These programs provide a method for you to hide your address from your abuser. They provide a generic mailing address to which your mail can be delivered and that you can use for most bills and other correspondence. This makes it more difficult for your abuser to find you. Again, your local crisis center should be able to tell you if your state or town has such a program. If not, you can consider renting a PO box under a different name that he wouldn't be able to track down.

Legal Issues

Have you felt overwhelmed by the various legal issues that have now become part of your life? If you have, you are not alone. Important legal matters are often part and parcel of the process of terminating abusive relationships. These include, but are not limited to obtaining and enforcing a restraining order, filing separation and divorce documents, dealing with child custody issues, tax assistance, establishing financial independence, and documenting the abuse for legal purposes. A more detailed discussion of these legal issues and obtaining help with them follows.

Obtaining Legal Help

You may feel you need legal help and advice, for some of the reasons discussed in the previous section, but have no idea how to find it and/or you doubt you can afford it. Fortunately, awareness of domestic violence issues within the legal community has created various avenues for obtaining competent legal advice and representation at low or no cost. You just need to know how to find those sources.

First, find out if there are any attorneys in your area who specialize in domestic violence work for reduced or no fees. If you do not find a listing in your local phone book under "Legal Aid," call your local crisis center. They should be able to guide you to available and affordable legal resources.

A national organization dedicated to providing assistance to victims of abuse is the **American Bar Association's (ABA) Commission on Domestic & Sexual Violence.** Its very informative Web site: (www.americanbar.org/groups/domestic_violence.html) provides phone numbers for abuse hotlines and lawyer referrals for all types of legal problems, state by state. Be careful when looking up any sort of help on a computer if you think there might ever be a chance your abuser will obtain access to it. Use a computer at work or your local library or a nearby college or university. The ABA Commission may also be reached by phone at 800-285-2221 (again, if your abuser has access to your phone, do not leave any trace of these contacts).

Many cities, counties, and law schools sponsor legal aid clinics. These clinics are staffed by advanced law students or practicing or retired lawyers who are volunteering their time and help. These clinics can be found in the yellow pages under "Legal Aid" or by calling a local law school or women's shelter. If you contact a legal aid clinic, be sure to ask for a volunteer who is specifically trained to handle domestic violence cases. Finally, you can obtain more information on sources for legal assistance from the National Domestic Violence Hotline at 1-800-799-SAFE.

Restraining Orders

You have probably heard of restraining orders (ROs), also called stay-away or protective orders. (These are discussed in Chapter 2, "Are You Out of Danger Now?") ROs are issued in an effort to stop your former partner from abusing, threatening, or interfering with you and your children.

A violation of the restraining order is a crime, and the police may arrest the abuser even if they did not witness the violation. Fear of arrest may be enough reason for some abusers to obey the order, but a restraining order is *no guarantee* of safety.

The exact characteristics of ROs, the details of obtaining them, and the specific penalties for violation vary somewhat from state to state. If you want someone to explain the process to you, your town's court personnel, your local crisis center staff, or a lawyer can assist you (also refer to womenslaw.org for more information on ROs in your state).

Other Court Proceedings

Separation and divorce papers can be extremely complicated and complex, especially when they involve property disputes or child custody issues. This process can feel even more overwhelming while recovering emotionally from your relationship. Typically, abusers will resist divorce proceedings, because they believe they will be able to coerce you back into the relationship.

If your abuser is the legal parent of the children, and the abuse cannot be proved legally, many courts will require some form of joint custody or visitation arrangement. This can be a frightening prospect when you know how abusive and dangerous your ex-partner can be. Once again, a crisis center advocate, counselor, or lawyer can help you through this process.

Financial–Legal Issues

Your abuser may have acquired sole access to all the family money. Abusers often use financial tactics to ensure their partner's complete dependency. You may find that none of your "joint" bank accounts and credit cards were in your name. On the other hand, some abusers do not contribute financially at all and require their partners to provide necessary income. If this was true in your relationship, you still may have had no say in any financial matters or even in how the money *you* earned was spent.

Untangling yourself financially from your abuser and establishing your economic independence can be a very complicated and confusing process. It may be especially tricky if you had little control or knowledge of your finances during the relationship. However, even if you knew a great deal about how your money was being spent, the debt that was being created, or any credit that was being established, the financial legacy of your relationship can be extremely complex and emotionally draining.

If you were married to your abuser, you may be liable for your ex's debts. Even if you were not married, abusers sometimes coerce their partners to cosign for loans and credit purchases. Moreover, you may have felt helpless to refuse to sign fraudulent joint tax returns during the relationship, placing you at risk for IRS actions if back taxes are owed. Legal procedures exist for separating your credit histories and establishing your own credit standing, but you will usually need the advice of a trained financial advisor or lawyer.

Criminal Charges

Finally, remember that relationship violence is sometimes a crime. In some cases, proving the violence occurred and demonstrating its severity is difficult. If prosecuting your abuser is an option, you will likely need a lawyer to help you make the strongest case possible for arrest, trial, conviction, and imprisonment.

Financial Assistance

If you are like many survivors who escape an abusive partner, you may have found yourself in a difficult financial situation. As mentioned above, your abuser may have tightly controlled the money in your relationship as part of the control over you, and when you left, you may have had no access to savings or checking accounts. Furthermore, you may not be employed, or the income from your job may seem insufficient to support you and your children. Worries about money should never force you to return to your abuser. Therefore, it is important for you to get back on your feet financially as soon as possible. Here are some suggestions for finding temporary financial help.

Friends and Family

Do you have friends or family who may be willing to help you out financially? Maybe some have already offered. This is probably a good time to ask for help or take them up on their offers. Many people feel embarrassed to accept money from others, but this is a time for you to focus on your emotional healing. Close friends and relatives are probably relieved you are out of that terrible situation and would really like to help you. If accepting a gift makes you too uncomfortable, agree to take the money as a loan and offer a written promise to repay it. Keep in mind that accepting help from others is not selfish or weak, but a frank acknowledgment of your current, *temporary* crisis.

Crisis Centers

What if you don't have people able to give or lend you money? There are several other possible routes you can take to smooth out your financial crisis. One source of help is your local crisis center. Crisis centers in your area may have information about where you can go to obtain some funding such as local town welfare, churches and/or government funds. Crisis centers may also, depending on your circumstances, be able to provide short-term shelter and support until you can find a source of income.

Finding Employment

If you do not have a job already and if your situation allows, you may want to consider obtaining work as soon as you can. Although this is often easier said than done, you might want to think about accepting a job that may not be your ideal choice just so you can begin to receive a check, and possibly some benefits. It is also a boost to your self-esteem and self-confidence to be working and bringing home a paycheck. You do not have to think of this as a permanent position; it can be just a job to help you get by until you can find something better.

Some survivors of abusive relationships have been denied the opportunity to develop job skills. This is another tactic abusers use to keep their partners wholly dependent on them. If you are in such a position, you might want to consider acquiring skills or obtaining some education toward a career that interests you. As long as you are earning enough to get by for now, you can take some time to cultivate your skills and talents. During this time of healing, you do not need to feel pressured to obtain a degree or to find your ideal career. Today, adults of all ages return to school—high school equivalency programs, community colleges, four-year colleges, and universities. You can approach your education slowly, even taking just one course at a time. Often financial aid is available for job training and education. Consider talking to the financial aid office of a local college or university.

In addition to their many counseling, support, and prevention services, most domestic violence crisis centers offer referrals to job training programs, including skills assessment, strategies for obtaining and keeping jobs, resume preparation, and job placement services with ties to potential employers in the community. They are there to help you, and sometimes the best course of action you can take is to let them do so.

Public Sources of Financial Assistance

Many governmental programs at the federal, state, and local levels are charged with helping survivors of domestic abuse and violence. At the federal and state levels these include public assistance benefits (welfare), food stamp programs, Medicaid benefits, Social Security Disability Insurance (SSDI) benefits, Supplemental Security Income (SSI) benefits, Temporary Assistance for Needy Families (TANF), and the federal welfare program for families with children. You may qualify for one or more of these programs.

Most state and local governments offer additional programs as well. It can sometimes be difficult to find these programs, to determine the ones for which you may qualify, and to fill out and submit the appropriate forms needed to receive the assistance. Domestic violence crisis centers have staff members who can help you apply for these programs. In addition, specific government offices in your town or county seat are in charge of administering these funds. Although they may not always offer personalized service, they can provide you with the forms and instructions you will need to begin the application process.

You may be hesitant to apply for public assistance because you perceive the social stigmas that are attached to being a "welfare recipient." But if you stop to think about it, these programs have been developed to help those who are in situations such as yours. You are not taking undue advantage of them. You are using them as they were intended to be used: to support you and your children while you are in transition from your old, unhealthy life to your new, productive one.

Reestablishing Credit

If the credit cards, loans, mortgage, and so forth were in your abuser's name, you may be in the position of needing to establish your own credit, starting from scratch. In today's economic environment, good credit is important for everything from obtaining a credit card to financing a car to buying a home. For most financial institutions, no credit history is the same as a bad one. Again, you can begin slowly to reestablish credit in your name. Lawyers and financial professionals who donate time and information to survivors of abuse are excellent resources for you in this regard. But you can take some steps on your own.

Many banks and credit unions offer *secured credit cards*. These are cards for which you deposit a specified amount, say, $300 or $500, into a savings account that serves as security for the credit card. The card's limit is the same as the amount you have placed on reserve. You use the card and make your monthly payments just as you would for any credit card. After a while, the bank sees that you are using the card responsibly and will convert the card to a standard credit account.

Other ways of establishing credit involve financing items from large retail stores. Often, department chain stores will offer credit more readily to its customers than will banks or credit unions. If it is within your budget to finance a major purchase (such as a TV or some furniture) and make all your payments on time, you will acquire a reference that will make future credit transactions easier.

Finally, car dealerships will usually extend financing to buyers who are without an extensive credit history. You may pay a higher interest rate than someone with a good credit history. However, if you can afford it, establishing your own credit through financing a car may be worthwhile.

Health Care

Access to medical care, including personal counseling, during this period of healing from your abusive relationship is very important. Many sources of stress exist in your life right now and you should not have to add doubts about affording or obtaining medical care to the list. Health care is especially important because the tension of rebuilding your life often takes a toll on you physically. You may also need attention for injuries sustained at the hands of your abuser. However, many survivors lose health care benefits when they leave the relationship because they were provided through the abuser's employer or because they needed to leave their job.

If you and your abuser are (or were) legally married, many states require that your ex continue to maintain health insurance benefits his policy provided you until such time as a final divorce settlement is completed. But because some abusers refuse this support, you may need to call on an attorney to assert your legal rights to medical insurance. Keep in mind, however, that your ex may be able to determine your whereabouts through insurance statements, so be careful.

Federal and state programs such as those discussed in the previous section, including Medicaid and SSI, will often provide coverage for medical care to those who qualify. Finally, if you have a medical emergency and have no insurance or ability to pay out of pocket, go to the emergency department at your local hospital. Hospitals will not refuse to treat emergencies regardless of the patient's insurance or financial status.

Accepting Help

As was mentioned earlier, this early time of transition in your life may call for setting personal pride aside in deciding how to obtain the temporary help you need to survive. Perceiving the offers of assistance discussed here as "handouts" or as "charity" and feeling too proud, embarrassed, or ashamed to accept them is understandable and very normal. However, allowing those who can help to do so may be an important part of your individual process of healing. You know reclaiming your life after abuse is not easy, and if individuals and organizations can make it a bit less difficult, take them up on their offers. Remember, they *want* to help and your need for their help is only temporary. Maybe one day, when your life is back in order, you can repay them by working to help others who are going through what you are experiencing now.

This chapter offers two exercises to help you deal with the practicalities of living on your own. This first one is simply an opportunity for you to explore some of your options for rebuilding your life, from a practical rather than emotional perspective. Of course, the practical and the emotional are interconnected, so when one improves, the other usually does as well. The first part of this exercise allows you to identify some of the practical needs you may be experiencing, and to think about some possible resources that may be available to you for meeting those needs. This can help you to feel more in control of these issues that may seem overwhelming to you.

1a. Safety: List the ways in which you feel unsafe, either from the dangers posed by your former abuser or from any other issues in your current life.

_____

_____

_____

1b. List sources of support and assistance that you could call on to help you feel and be safer.

_____

_____

_____

2a. Legal issues: List what, if any, legal problems you anticipate now that you are out of the abusive relationship.

_____

_____

_____

2b. List the resources in your area that may be able to provide legal assistance with these issues.

_____

_____

_____

3a. Finances: List what, if any, financial problems you anticipate now that you are out of the abusive relationship.

_____

_____

3b. List the potential sources of financial help you may be able to access if money is a problem.

_____

_____

_____

4. Health care: List your possible sources for obtaining health care for you and, if applicable, for your children.

_____

_____

5. Education and career training: List some of the possible routes you might take to further your education and/or obtain the skills you need for a job or career path that is desirable to you.

_____

_____

_____

Just How Much Money Do You Need to Survive?

This next exercise may seem a bit mundane compared to others in this book, but it is certainly no less important. If you can calculate approximately how much money you actually need on a monthly basis to survive at a basic level, it will be clearer to you what you must focus on for salary and financial assistance in various forms. So on the budget below estimate an amount for each item that applies to you (enter $0 for the items that do not apply, or that you can do without). Be realistic! Don't underestimate, but focus on basic needs. This is a very detailed budget list so you will have as accurate an estimation as possible.

After you have estimated your monthly financial needs, there is another form to help you calculate your current and potential monthly income from various sources. These two basic pieces of information are necessary for you to make a plan that will lead to independence and self-sufficiency.

Budget Item	Estimated Monthly Expense
Grocery Store	
Groceries	$_____.00
Toiletries	$_____.00
Other _____	$ _____.00
Medical	
Hospital	$_____.00
Physician	$_____.00
Dentist	$_____.00
Prescriptions/vitamins	$_____.00
Health insurance	$_____.00
Other _____	$_____.00

Budget Item	Estimated Monthly Expense	

Transportation

Public transportation $_____.00

Car payments $_____.00

Taxes and fees $_____.00

Tolls $_____.00

Gas $_____.00

Auto maintenance $_____.00

Auto insurance $_____.00

Parking $_____.00

Parking permits $_____.00

Other _____ $_____.00

Clothing

Dry cleaning/laundry $_____.00

New purchases/personal $_____.00

New purchases/work $_____.00

Other _____ $_____.00

Education (You or Child)

Education/training expenses $_____.00

Registration fees $_____.00

Tuition $_____.00

Books $_____.00

Room and board $_____.00

Miscellaneous $_____.00

Other _____ $_____.00

Budget Item	**Estimated Monthly Expense**

Child Expenses

Day care	$_____.00
Babysitting	$_____.00
Clothing	$_____.00
Diapers	$_____.00
Formula	$_____.00
Medicines	$_____.00
Special food items (baby food)	$_____.00
Other _____	$_____.00

Work Related

Meals	$_____.00
Office supplies	$_____.00
Uniforms	$_____.00
Union dues	$_____.00
Other _____	$_____.00

Home Expenses

Mortgage or rent	$_____.00
Gas	$_____.00
Electric	$_____.00
Heat	$_____.00
Water	$_____.00
Sewer	$_____.00
Insurance	$_____.00
Maintenance	$_____.00
Property tax	$_____.00
Snow plowing	$_____.00
Average phone use	$_____.00
Other _____	$_____.00

Budget Item	Estimated Monthly Expense
Fixed Monthly Bills	
Credit card payments	$_____.00
Loan payments	$_____.00
Other _____	$_____.00
Pets	
Vet bills	$_____.00
Food	$_____.00
Board and care	$_____.00
Other _____	$_____.00
Monthly Pocket Money Allowance	$_____.00
Total Estimated Minimum Monthly Expenses	$_____.00

Current and Potential Sources of Income

OK, now you'll need to think about the sources for the money in your budget. Using the chart below, estimate as realistically as possible the amount you receive from current sources and the total amount you could probably receive if you were to make use of other possible resources such as those discussed in this chapter. Comparing these amounts with your basic needs will help you focus your priorities on meeting your basic needs on your own, independent of your abusive partner.

Source	Current Amount	Potential Amount Available
Job(s)	$_____.00	$_____.00
From savings	$_____.00	$_____.00
Child support	$_____.00	$_____.00
Alimony	$_____.00	$_____.00
From family	$_____.00	$_____.00
From friends	$_____.00	$_____.00
Public assistance (SSI, TANF, etc.)	$_____.00	$_____.00
Other sources of income (list):		
_____	$_____.00	$_____.00
_____	$_____.00	$_____.00
_____	$_____.00	$_____.00
Totals	$_____.00	$_____.00

13

Beginning to Heal

Myth: With enough effort, anyone can figure out solutions to their problems on their own.

Myth: If you need professional therapy, you must be crazy.

Myth: If you are strong enough, you can overcome anything on your own.

You may be wondering when you will finally respond with an *honest* "Fine!" when someone asks, "How are you?" As you are beginning to build your new life, you will probably need to confront some of the troubling emotions that are plaguing you.

Typically, three of the most overwhelming emotions among survivors are anger, depression, and anxiety. If these emotions become too severe, they can consume your life and derail your recovery.

Anger

Nothing is intrinsically wrong with anger. Anger is a normal, healthy emotion. You have every right to feel anger toward your abuser. But if you feel the anger might be getting the better of you, it might be time to evaluate your anger and take some steps to gain some control over it.

How often are you angry? Is it interfering with your relationships with others? Is your anger always just below the surface, threatening to trigger negative thoughts and feelings? Do you find you obsess about how you might be able to get back at your abuser? If so, your anger may have reached the point where it may damage your well-being if you don't learn to manage it.

If you feel you are angry all the time or if you are having any thoughts of *actually* injuring, maiming, or killing your abuser, you need to seek immediate help. Attacking your former abuser will only make your life worse and hurt others who love you. It's important to remind yourself that your ex just isn't worth it.

Most people learn as children that yelling, hitting, and destroying property are wrong. But at times, these behaviors, if performed in therapeutic, directed, and harmless ways, can help vent some of your stored-up anger.

If you ever feel you are so angry you want to scream, perhaps that's just what you should do. Find a place where no one will hear, and yell and scream as long as you want. Say whatever you are feeling. Don't hold back. Say everything you were never able to say to your abuser. Express how angry you are about what happened to you, about all that was taken from you. Consider inviting a trusted, understanding friend to join you. If you feel exhausted or tearful after this release, your friend can help you safely home.

If you don't have access to a place to yell, try screaming into a pillow. You might feel silly at first, but if you let yourself go, it will work wonders in ridding yourself of the accumulated rage. Yelling isn't a cure-all, but it can provide a safe emotional release.

Do you have times when you feel so angry you just want to hit someone? Hitting anyone, especially your former abuser, will only make the situation worse for you and could be dangerous. If you feel the need to hit, it's important to find ways of expressing this desire without causing yourself more harm. Hitting your bed or punching pillows can help release some of your fury. Hit something soft that will not hurt your hands. Striking a wall or door will only injure you and you have been hurt enough. You may want to consider investing in a punching bag (they can be purchased in a variety of sizes and prices).

Are you able to express your angry thoughts or do you repress them? Every time you feel the anger surfacing, do you push it down and force yourself to think about something else? If you haven't been able to let the angry thoughts out, try writing them down. Write everything that is causing your anger. If anger is an uncomfortable emotion for you, this may be difficult at first. Take it slowly if it helps. Start by writing the one or two angry thoughts that come up most frequently. At first, these may be general issues such as, "I'm angry about the abuse" or "I'm furious at my abuser!" As you continue to work on your list, you can refine or add to them and make them much more specific. For example, specific anger-producing thoughts might include, "I'm furious you imprisoned me by following me everywhere I went!" or "I hate you for breaking my favorite vase!"

Eventually, try to write down everything that makes you angry. When you feel you are finished with your list for now, consider what you want to do with it. If you feel this has relieved much of your anger, you may want to put your list away for future reference. However, if you would rather get rid of this list, you might consider some therapeutic methods of disposing of it.

Take some time deciding what method of destroying your anger list will feel most cleansing. You can get rid of it all at once or in pieces. If you want to get rid of it all at once, try creating an anger-purging ceremony. You may want to make a statement or recite a poem you wrote expressing your feelings. On the other hand, you may want your feelings to pour out spontaneously. Your ceremony may involve tearing the list into as many small pieces as possible. You may then want to burn or bury the pieces. Whatever you decide to do, the idea of this ritual is to help you release your anger safely and liberate yourself from that rage.

If you think it would be more helpful for you to let go of the angry thoughts gradually, you may want to destroy parts of your list over time. One method of asserting your anger is to write one or more items from your anger list on pieces of tape. Stick the tape to the bottom of your shoes. Throughout the day, let your anger out by stomping your foot, walking especially hard, or by stepping into something you would normally avoid. Or, perhaps you want to tape items from your list onto each foot and do a "dance of healing." Be as creative as you want. Being physical with anger can bring welcome release.

Depression

Many common symptoms of depression are discussed in Chapter 8, "When Feelings Overwhelm You." Some of the all-important signs of depression include continuous sadness, changes in your eating and sleeping patterns, fatigue, feelings of hopelessness, and thoughts of hurting or killing yourself. Depressive symptoms may appear or intensify in the aftermath of an abusive relationship.

Mild Depression

How did you rate the various elements of depression in Part III of the *Self-Exploration* exercise at the end of Chapter 8, "When Feelings Overwhelm You"? If your ratings in that part of the exercise generally fell between 1 and 4, you may be somewhat depressed, but your mood probably isn't interfering seriously with your daily life or relationships with others. It probably feels manageable, although certainly not pleasurable. These are signs of mild depression. If your depression is mild, you can choose to take action to ease your sadness or you can wait for it to lift on its own. If you choose to deal actively with your depression, here are some effective ways to help soothe the pain.

One method of alleviating mild depression is to verbalize your sadness. Sometimes, merely expressing your emotions to someone who is supportive and will really listen can work wonders. Talking with a trusted friend or family member about your feelings can be very effective in easing the depression. If you are lacking the support you need at this time in your life, it's time to work on rebuilding those human resources of strength. You may perhaps be able to find support from family, friends, neighbors, or coworkers. But if not, consider joining a local club, organization, or church group, or becoming involved in volunteer work. These activities, besides being fun and building your self-esteem, can assist you in meeting new people. Isolation and loneliness will usually intensify depression.

Another important part of coping with depression is to learn to accept your feelings. Emotions are not right or wrong. If you are hiding from your emotions, not allowing yourself to feel, you could be making the depression worse. Hiding your true feelings will not make them go away.

Again, try writing down all the reasons why you feel depressed. Acknowledge that what you have been through is more than sufficient reason to feel the way you do. Allow yourself to feel down, cry, and do whatever you need to do to be in touch with your emotions.

At the same time, make a point of doing something pleasurable for yourself every day. Start an exercise program, take a bubble bath, go for a long walk in the woods, talk with a friend on the phone, read a magazine, or work on an art or craft project. Be sure to allow yourself the pleasure of these activities on a regular basis. Your depression might blunt some of the pleasure in these activities for a while, but treat yourself to them anyway because they, in turn, will help defeat your depression.

Moderate or Severe Depression

If your scores in Part III of the Self-Exploration exercise in Chapter 8 generally fell above 4, this suggests that your depression may be moderate to severe. You may want to focus on more aggressive treatment. After an abusive relationship ends, depression is normal, but you shouldn't have to live with it forever. You can decide to get some help and start feeling better.

How do you know when your depression is serious enough to require additional help? You are usually the best judge of that. Follow your instincts. Even if you're not sure whether or not you need counseling, consider seeing someone who can help you decide. Some general guidelines may help you determine just how serious your depression is and if you might need some professional help.

A key sign of more serious depression is that it is interfering noticeably with your daily activities. Are you finding it difficult to go to work or to perform up to your usual standards while on the job? Are routine tasks such as making meals, taking care of your children, or maintaining your home beginning to feel overwhelming? Do you no longer find enjoyment in your favorite activities? These are indications the depression is worsening.

It's also important to pay attention to your sleeping and eating patterns. Sleeping too much, sleeping very little, or awakening very early in the morning without being able to go back to sleep are symptoms of serious depression. If you are eating very little, or are eating much more than your usual amount, these may be signs that the depression is becoming more significant.

Suicidal Thoughts

Probably the most alarming sign of serious depression involves thoughts of hurting or killing yourself. Do you have days when you wish you would just not wake up the next morning? Do you sometimes "hope" an accident will relieve you of the burden of going on? At times, do you feel everyone would be better off if you were out of the picture? These thoughts should alert you to keep a very close eye on your depression. *If you begin to feel you might actually act on these thoughts, you need to get help immediately.* If you find yourself actually planning to kill yourself, thinking of methods you might use to kill yourself, or contemplating the "right time" to kill yourself, you should get help *now*. Tell a friend, a family member, your doctor, or see a counselor, but don't wait until it's too late.

If you are experiencing symptoms of moderate or serious depression, it might not be the kind of problem you can overcome on your own. Seeking therapy does not mean that you are weak or crazy. You are having a normal reaction to a traumatic past. Obtaining counseling simply means you understand you are unable to work through all of your difficulties alone and are ready to allow a trained, caring professional to guide you through them. Later in this chapter, we will discuss how you can find someone to help you.

Anxiety

Everyone suffers from anxiety from time to time. When unexpected or uncontrollable events occur, we often feel anxious and worry about how everything will turn out. These normal feelings of anxiety are temporary and usually do not interfere with our lives in significant or long-term ways.

Some forms of anxiety, however, can be serious and debilitating. Often, you can identify a serious anxiety problem because the anxiety begins to take over. It is controlling you instead of you controlling it. This kind of anxiety often manifests itself in your interactions with others. Mild to moderate anxiety often causes one to be irritable and curt with others. You may appear more on edge and jumpy. Others may tell you to relax, "chill out," but you know that is easier said than done. You try to tell yourself to stop worrying so much, but if that works at all, it's a temporary fix.

If you feel your abuser continues to pose a real threat and you are concerned about protecting yourself and your children, you have a right to be anxious. You are being realistic and smart. But what if physical safety is not a concern? Does this mean that you don't "have a right" to be anxious? Of course not. Even if physical violence was never a part of your relationship, you may still feel anxious for many reasons now that you're out. If nothing else, starting your life over is enough to make anyone terribly anxious.

Extreme anxiety can also affect your mental processes. It can cause you to become stuck in a vicious cycle in which your attempt to stop your negative thoughts causes them to spin around and around in your mind even faster. You may find yourself feeling help-less and hopeless: "I can't do that," "Things will never work out," or "It's all just too much for me." These are signs that your anxiety might be getting the better of you.

Anxiety also affects people physically. Do you have frequent stomachaches, neck or back pain, or headaches? Do you seem to get sick with colds and flu more than most people? Do you have fre-quent episodes of diarrhea or constipation? Does your heart race? Do you break out in cold sweats or hyperventilate? These can be signs of more serious anxiety.

Severe anxiety can lead to very frightening episodes called *panic attacks*. Symptoms of panic attacks include shortness of breath, rapid heart rate, profuse sweating, tunnel vision, feelings of having a heart attack, a sense of "unreality," and even the perception of impending death.

Nothing is wrong or crazy about suffering from anxiety. You are dealing with difficult, painful, and often frightening issues. Anxiety is one of many signs that you need to continue to heal from the abuse you suffered. If you feel the need, trained counselors can help you learn to reduce and cope with your anxiety.

Getting Help

When we talk about "getting help" or seeking the assistance of a "trained professional," we are referring to meeting with a counselor or therapist who specializes in working with individuals who have been in abusive relationships. Many people resist the idea of psychotherapy, believing "only crazy people need that." But that is far from the truth. Psychotherapy offers help for "non-crazy" psychological or emotional problems, such as excessive anger, depression, or anxiety.

How can you tell if you should seek professional psychological help? For one thing, getting help does *not* mean you are "mentally ill." On the contrary, the vast majority of those seeking psychotherapy do not have a mental illness, but are simply experiencing painful problems in their lives that they are unable to solve on their own. For many, however, because of society's erroneous beliefs and stigmas, deciding to get help for emotional pain can be a more difficult decision than seeking medical care.

When you are physically sick or injured you usually experience relatively clear symptoms that serve as guidelines for calling the doctor. If you twist your knee skiing, the amount and duration of pain, swelling, discoloration, and loss of use will guide you in your decision whether or not to seek medical attention. Emotional problems may be just as painful, but most people are unclear what clues indicate a need for counseling.

How can you tell when the emotions you are feeling in the aftermath of an abusive relationship are "serious enough" to get help? As we've discussed throughout this chapter, if you analyze the intensity, duration, and the extent to which the emotions are interfering with your present life and future goals, you should be able to tell if you would benefit from counseling.

Many sources for psychological support are available, some of which may be inexpensive or even free. You can obtain a referral from your local crisis center or physician. You can also talk to people at your church, or ask friends and relatives who may have sought therapy themselves. If you are taking at least one class at a college or university, personal counseling services are often available there. *However, be sure that you find a counselor who is knowledgeable about and trained in helping survivors of controlling and abusive relationships.*

Psychotherapy works. Counselors, social workers, therapists, and psychologists are trained to help you deal with your anger, overcome your depression, and control your anxiety. Many people do not need to continue in therapy for years and years. In fact, progress can often be made in fewer than ten sessions. Counseling is something you do for yourself. It is *completely* confidential. No one else ever needs to know what you said during sessions with a counselor or even that you are seeing someone. You may feel uncomfortable and a little frightened making that first appointment, but getting the help you need is an important step toward healing.

Do You Need Professional Help?

This exercise is designed to help you decide if you want to consider counseling. Take your time as you go through this checklist. Be honest with yourself. You will only be limiting yourself by "fudging" the answers.

The more frequent the feelings and behaviors and the more checks you see when you are done, the greater the potential benefits from counseling. (**Note: If you are having any suicidal thoughts, you should seek professional help immediately.**) If you decide to seek therapy, you can also use this exercise anytime during your counseling process for a clear assessment of your progress.

We recommend that you make copies of this exercise and complete the checklist now, about one month from now, and perhaps each month or so after that. At these various points, you may well see improvement. If you do not see a decrease in the frequency of your painful emotions, that might be a useful signal to either seek or continue with professional counseling.

Emotional Behavior as of: (Date) _____	Check the Frequency of Your Behavior				
	Very Often	Often	Once-in-a-While	Almost Never	Never
Angry verbal outbursts					
Feeling enraged					
Throwing things					
Hitting things					
Feeling hopeless					
Feeling helpless					
Changes in sleeping					
Changes in eating					
Feeling sad and "blue"					
Thoughts of self-injury					
Hitting people**					
Self-injurious actions**					
Suicide attempts**					
Suicidal thoughts**					
Excessive worrying					
Headaches					
Stomach/digestion problems					
Neck aches					
Backaches					
Anxiety					
Panic attacks					
Other _____					
Other _____					

**Please note:* If the items marked ** are checked in any column except "never," you should seek counseling immediately regardless of your overall score on this exercise.

Interpreting Your Ratings

No single test can comprehensively assess your need for counseling. Your score on this *Self-Exploration* exercise is just one factor in your decision to seek professional help at this complicated time in your life. Obviously the more frequently you suffer from any of the behaviors and feelings in the scale, the more likely it is that some professional counseling is needed to help you deal with them effectively.

Pay special attention to each item you checked *very often* or *often*. You are probably experiencing a great deal of pain from these feelings or behaviors. Most likely, your healing process will require some professional counseling sooner rather than later. These issues may be troubling you a great deal and, unless you can move toward resolving them, they could interfere with your successful healing process.

Also, notice the overall number of items you have rated in the most frequent three columns. If you see many of these, say, five or more, you may find it difficult to get through all of them on your own. The sheer number of these issues is another indication that some professional assistance might be very helpful to you in reducing the frequency of your unproductive feelings and behaviors and coping with your life in general.

Now, consider the items you rated as *almost never* or *never*. With the exception of the items marked with ** as noted earlier, these items are probably giving you little or no trouble at all. You probably have little need for professional counseling for these issues at this time. As time passes, and your healing process continues, you should find more and more of your troubling feelings and behaviors moving over into the *never* column.

Finally, remember, if your score on this scale indicates that your emotions are fairly well in check, but you feel a need for some professional help nonetheless, *follow your instincts*.

After a month or so, complete this *Self-Exploration* exercise again (remember: If you are having any suicidal thoughts, you should seek professional help immediately).

Compare your scores with your results from the previous month. You should see a decrease in the overall frequency of your troubling feelings and behaviors. That is, you should see the behaviors you rated as *very often* or *often*, beginning to move down to the *once-in-a-while*, *almost never*, or *never* columns and more of the *once-in-a-while* or *almost never* items now checked in the *never* category.

If you do not see any improvement, or your painful feelings and behaviors are becoming *more* frequent, this may be an important sign for you to seek out or to continue some professional counseling. Some counseling with a therapist trained in abuse issues or with advocates at a local crisis center can help you to move past these issues and continue on your path of healing.

Finally, as we have said before, if your score on this scale indicates that you're doing OK with handling your emotions, but you feel you could use some professional help nonetheless, *follow your instincts.*

14

Who Are You Now?

Myth: After an abusive relationship, you will immediately feel great about yourself.

Myth: Believing in yourself just comes naturally when you are free from your abuser.

Myth: It's easy to know who you are after you get out of an abusive relationship.

*T*he power and control your abuser used were based on a number of factors: his belief that he had the right to treat you as his property and treat you in any way he wanted, and his decision to abuse you and have control over every aspect of your life. One method he most likely also employed was to make you believe that you didn't deserve anything better.

In the beginning of the relationship your ex might have made you feel that he adored everything about you. You may have felt that in his eyes you could do no wrong. Unfortunately, over time this gradually changed. Your ex most likely slowly started finding fault with little things here and there. He may have begun by saying they were no big deal. Over time, however, he began to consistently comment on these "faults" and began to make it seem as though you were unworthy. Your abuser worked consistently and relentlessly to make you feel unworthy. Over time, his comments and innuendos caused your self-esteem to take nose dive. Now even after you are out of that abusive relationship, you still may have poor self-esteem.

For some survivors, particularly if they experienced abuse or neglect in their childhood or in past relationships may have gone into this relationship with poor self-esteem. If this was the case, your ex most likely picked up on this and knew exactly what to say and how to act to get right to the heart of your insecurities.

How would you describe yourself to a stranger, someone you've never met and who knows nothing about you? Think how you would answer if the stranger asked you to be as detailed as possible and include both the positive and negative in your self-description? Which list would be longer, your "pluses" or your "minuses"? Do you like who you are? Do you believe you deserve the best from life? Do you have some valuable skills and abilities? Or do you feel somewhat worthless and unworthy of life's gifts?

Assessing Your Current Self-Concept

As silly as these questions sound, they are a way to begin to assess your current level of self-esteem. Self-esteem is complicated. It's composed of many ingredients that determine how you judge yourself. Healthy self-esteem implies that you see yourself as a person who has as much right to happiness and satisfaction in life as anyone else.

If you have not paid attention to your self-esteem, it may be time to start. Make a list of your unique, healthy, and outstanding attributes. Include all the qualities that make you a good person and the traits you especially like about yourself. Your list might include central self-concepts such as honesty, your sense of humor, your trusting nature, or your sensitivity to the feelings of others. It can also contain some outward characteristics such as your laugh, the shape of your nose, or the way you dance.

Did you find it difficult to complete your list? If you are like most survivors of abuse, you haven't spent much time thinking about your good qualities. While you were in that relationship, it may have been no time at all. All too often, survivors of abusive relationships completely forget how wonderful they are.

Was it uncomfortable for you to list your positive attributes? Did you feel embarrassed, afraid someone might see it and think you were terribly vain? Believing in yourself does not mean you are conceited or arrogant. It means you like yourself, that's all, and that's good.

Who You Were Before the Abuse

It's not always true that your life would be terrific if only you hadn't suffered through that relationship. Is it possible that your life was not exactly perfect before the abuse?

As you begin to heal and change your life, think about when your current difficulties began. How did you feel about yourself before your abusive relationship? Were you a confident, self-assured individual with a positive and healthy self-concept? Did you see yourself as a good friend, a good partner, a loving parent, a productive worker? How much time did you spend taking care of yourself and *your* needs versus taking care of others? Were you as good to yourself as to everyone else in your life? Or were you more likely to care for others and neglect yourself?

Perhaps your self-esteem was healthy before the relationship and it was the abuse that caused you to lose faith in yourself. On the other hand, however, you may have had a less-than-positive self-image long before the abuse. For some survivors, self-esteem and self-confidence problems didn't begin with the abuse, the abuse only made them worse. Many people suffer from low self-esteem and often the causes for this are unclear. A person's upbringing, family dynamics, culture, friends, and peers all play a significant role in his or her self-concept as an adult. So, in your process of becoming a fully functioning person, it will help to recognize any past influences you may need to work on as you heal from the abuse.

Those Criticizing Voices in Your Head

Do you ever feel as though little voices inside your head are saying you are not good enough? Maybe a voice says, "Who are you to think that you can..." or "Oh, sure, like *you* could ever succeed at..." Have you ever thought about whose voice it is? Maybe it's time to do that.

The next time you sense one of those belittling or degrading voices, think about who said those words to you. You will probably think of your abuser first, but were there others in your past who made you feel you were not good enough? Who was it that seemed to have nothing but negative comments no matter what you did or how hard you tried? Who was it who reacted to your accomplishments with silence; no criticisms, perhaps, but no compliments or praise either? Did someone offer support in some ways, but in other areas constantly put you down? Who was it that picked you apart?

Your abuser probably embodied all these people. Looking back on the insults and humiliations, it's easy to see how you were made to lose faith in yourself. To your abuser, it was necessary to "break your spirit" and make you feel unworthy. Destroying your self-esteem was a very powerful strategy for controlling you.

However, long before that relationship came onto the scene, maybe others set the stage for your poor self-esteem. Now, in the process of learning to love yourself and becoming a strong, self-assured person, looking at all of these influences is essential.

Hearing Your Abuser's Voice

Throughout this book we have been talking about the ways in which your abuser's behavior was designed, in part, to destroy your self-esteem. It's imperative for you to remind yourself frequently why your ex said those terrible things to you. All of the verbal, psychological, and physical abuse was calculated to control you. To the extent that you could be convinced of your unworthiness, your partner's hold over you was strengthened. And abusers are very good at it: they know exactly which buttons to push. They identify their victim's most insecure areas, where their self-esteem is already a little shaky, and zero in on them. However, all those insulting and degrading comments were not really about you. They were about your abuser's pathological need for control.

Realizing and remembering the true purpose of all the put-downs and slurs is crucial for healing. Every time you hear that voice in your head, remind yourself those words were totally unjustified. Even if you see a grain of truth in some of them, keep in mind your abuser was exaggerating them, using them as a weapon against you. For example, your abuser may have set up impossible expectations and when you could not or would not meet them, you would hear accusations of being unreliable and untrustworthy. But this was your ex's problem, not yours. However, now that you are out and no longer controlled, you may still see yourself as thoughtless or undependable. If so, that's your abuser's voice still exerting some control over you.

The truth is that no one is perfect and it's unfair to expect that of yourself, even if your abuser expected it of you. You may *want* to change some aspects of yourself and that's healthy. All of us have characteristics or behaviors we would like to change. But just because you want to change does not mean you are not a good person right now.

When It's Not Your Abuser's Voice

If the derogatory voice running through your mind sometimes belongs to someone from your life before the abusive relationship (such as your mother, father, an older sibling, a friend, etc.) you need to pay attention to it. Anyone who diminished your self-esteem while you were growing up may have created a difficult and long-lasting burden.

Recognizing that someone from your past helped to create your negative self-concepts does not mean you now have to hate, blame, or confront that person. What it does mean is that you need to work through those issues. For you to discover that a friend or family member undermined your self-esteem can be very painful. Even if they had no intention of causing you to think less of yourself, they did. Many reasons may help explain why friends or family members are not always supportive and encouraging. Usually, they don't realize the impact of their words and actions. They may have thought they were making you a stronger person by "telling you the truth" as they saw it. Or putting you down may have made them feel "bigger." Maybe they were treating you as they were treated when growing up. Whatever the reason, as you work on healing from the abuse, you need to consider how they affected your self-esteem.

Perhaps you are feeling influenced by voices, other than your abuser's, from the time *during* the abuse? Maybe you still hear the echoes of those people who tried to tell you, directly or indirectly, that the abuse was your fault or you were nuts to stay as long as you did. Many reasons for their actions are discussed in Chapter 11, "The Reactions of Others." Their opinions and comments were probably due to ignorance of abusive relationships or the fact that they were deceived by the charm and outward facade of your abuser. They were not seeing the truth of your life. If you keep their comments in perspective you can help yourself to let go of them.

Purging the Voices from Your Past

If you could find some understandable reason why a friend or family member treated you so poorly, letting go of the negative beliefs they caused might be easier. But if you seem unable to find such an explanation, you may feel as if their voices will haunt you forever.

Usually, ridding yourself of those voices from the past involves recognizing the harmful thoughts they created in your mind and working to change them. You will need time to place those voices in their proper perspective. Once you understand the true motives behind the voices, remind yourself often that the words are false. You need not allow them to cause you pain any longer.

It may also be very helpful to talk with trusted members of your family or others who were with you when these old relationships existed (see the *Self-Exploration* exercise at the end of this chapter). Discuss with them your perception of what happened back then and how you felt. You may hear something such as, "I know exactly what you mean. I felt the same thing!" Knowing you were not alone then and are not alone now can be wonderfully comforting. You may also find that others may be able to give you new insights into those past events. This new knowledge may accelerate the process of eliminating the old, painful voices.

If nothing works and those voices continue to affect your self-image, it may be time to seek some professional help to silence them once and for all (see Chapter 13, "Beginning to Heal").

When the Voice Is Yours

Have you assumed your abuser's role of belittling yourself? Do you treat yourself with less respect and caring than you deserve? Sometimes, if someone else puts you down, insults, and degrades you for long enough, you begin to believe it's true. The controlling judgments begin to eat away at your self-image. Over time, that voice evolves into yours. Your abuser may be gone, that voice may have faded, but in your mind, you still hear the words—in your own voice. When this happens, self-defeating mental comments have the greatest power over you. If the critical voice is yours, you may need some extra time and work to "unlearn" these unhealthy beliefs. It's time to begin to treat *yourself* with dignity and approval.

Who Are You?

The first step toward increasing your self-esteem is rediscovering who you really are. The following exercise is designed to help you look at your character, personality, values, and overall human qualities. List as many of your personal positive characteristics as you can for each item on the list. Add as much detail as possible. If you find that you get "stuck" in a particular area, leave it blank for now, but keep it in mind over the next month or so. As you go about your daily life, try to uncover your positive characteristics that fit into the various categories, and when you do, add them to your lists.

As we suggest in other chapters' *Self-Explorations*, this exercise is designed to be repeated over time as you heal. Chapter 15, "The Temptation to Go Back," will help you to further assess and work on increasing your self-esteem. Be sure to come back to this and the exercises in Chapter 15 and *fill out them out again a month from now*. After you have completed the exercise for the second time, compare the two lists. If your lists are similar and you feel you are still lacking positive attributes in any category, you have more work to do on your self-esteem. If, on the other hand, your second list contains a lot more positive qualities, you are heading in the right direction as you reclaim your self-confidence and self-esteem.

Professional skills (hard worker, conscientious, dedicated, team player, etc.)

_____

_____

_____

Interpersonal skills (good listener, communicates thoughts and feelings well, giving, etc.)

_____

_____

_____

Values and ethics (honest, trustworthy, spiritual, etc.)

_____

_____

_____

Positive outlook (optimistic, upbeat, sense of humor, etc.)

_____

_____

_____

Yourself in relation to the world (concerned about others' feelings, environmentally conscious, kind to animals, etc.)

_____

_____

_____

Others (list)

_____

_____

_____

Remember, repeat this exercise in about a month. Analyze the changes you see, if any, over those four weeks. You can fill out this _Self-Exploration_ exercise whenever you want to keep tabs on your progress in this area.

SELF-EXPLORATION II

Unhealthy Influences in Your Life

This exercise may feel uncomfortable because you may not want to be critical of people in your life whom you liked, loved, or are related to. But, if your self-worth, self-image, or self-esteem was diminished by the way others have treated you, getting specific about it can be both therapeutic and healing. And, remember, no one has to see this except you.

How Did They Make You Feel About YOU

People in Your Life	How He or She Contributed or Detracted from Your Self-Esteem
Mother	
Father	
Brother(s)	
Sister(s)	
Friend 1	
Friend 2	
Friend 3	
A Teacher	
A Coach	
Your Abuser	
Add Another Person	
Add Another Person	

This exercise will help you determine where in your life were the biggest influences on your self-esteem, both positive and negative. This will place your abuser's tactics (how he used your weaknesses) and effects (why his tactics were so successful on you) in clearer perspective.

15

The Temptation to Go Back

Myth: Once survivors leave their abusive relationship, obviously they would never consider returning to their abusers.

Myth: Any survivor who returns to an abusive partner is weak and probably cannot survive independently.

Myth: If a survivor leaves the relationship and then goes back, any further abuse is the survivor's fault.

You know how difficult it was for you to leave your abuser. You know all the reasons you left: fear, humiliation, loss of self-esteem, isolation, physical danger, and so on. For all those reasons you changed your life and escaped from the constant control. Ultimately, only you can decide whether to go back. Should you find yourself considering returning to that relationship, this chapter is designed to help you make an informed, mindful decision. *We are by no means recommending that you go back.* Rather, we are saying that if you ever do think about going back, you should do so with your eyes wide open.

Anyone who has not endured an abusive relationship may find it very difficult to understand how you could consider, even for a moment, returning to your abuser. If you are contemplating returning and have attempted to discuss it with friends or family, they probably reacted with shock, disbelief, anger, and recriminations. Ironically, you may find yourself in the position of having only your ex to confide in about this difficult decision.

As we have discussed frequently in this book, reconstructing your life after an abusive relationship is never easy. Your new existence contains so many new sources of stress, apprehension, and doubt. You feel a very real sense of loss. Missing the positive aspects of your life in that relationship is completely understandable. The awful, painful, and traumatic events may not completely erase the good times. And now and then it may seem easier just to go back.

Feelings such as these do not in any way indicate that you should return. They are a normal part of the recovery process. However, all survivors must weigh the pros and cons of returning and decide the best course of action. It's OK to *think* about it. You are in control of your life now, and it's up to you to make the best choices for your life.

Weighing the Pros and Cons

As with any major decision, it's a good idea to examine your options thoroughly. Making a list is often very helpful. List all the pros and cons of going back and all the pros and cons of staying out of the relationship.

Begin by writing the positive characteristics of the relationship such as financial security, having an intimate partner, owning a home, and so on. Next, write down your ex-partner's positive traits such as a sense of humor, interests you shared, physical appearance, or any other characteristics you liked. Take your time with these lists. Do not hurry through them. If you need to, write a little, put them away for a while, then go back and add additional items later.

When you have your list of the positive factors, move on to the next list: the negatives. List all the painful, humiliating, frightening, and traumatic events during your time with your abuser. Include events such as the incidents of physical abuse, times when your abuser humiliated or embarrassed you in front of others, or controlled your whereabouts, friends, schedules, and activities. Next, list all of the negative personal characteristics of your former partner. Try to concentrate on the attributes that were damaging or harmful to you then and probably would be again if you were to go back. Items on this list might include your ex-partner's irrational jealousy, controlling nature, violent tendencies, or treating you as his property. Finally, include the basic human needs and desires that were lacking in that relationship such as, respect, emotional security, trust, or a violence-free life. List all the factors that made you leave.

Understandably, making these pro-and-con lists may be painful for you. Keep reminding yourself that you are out now and growing stronger. It is your decision to go back or not. No one else can tell you what is best for you. Reviewing your responses to the *Self-Exploration* exercises in Chapters 1 and 4 ("Were You in an Abusive Relationship" and "The Hidden Horror: Sexual Abuse") may assist you in completing your lists.

After you have finished your lists, examine them carefully. What do you see? Do the effects of the pros or the cons carry more weight in your life? You may need to give this careful thought before you seriously consider making another major change in your life. Deciding impulsively and without thorough deliberation could lead to more pain, violence, and heartache.

If you struggle repeatedly with thoughts of returning, your pro-and-con lists may come in handy more than once. Each time you are considering going back, review them, and if you need to, add or subtract items from either side of the list.

Reviewing Why You Left

You might find it helpful to reconsider why you left in the first place. You left because you were being abused. You left because you were afraid. You left because your life and your dignity had been taken from you. Remember the terrible difficulty you had getting out of the relationship? Remember how long and how much planning it took?

You may believe things would be different now. Your ex may be telling you how different and better your life together could be now (in much the same pattern that may have followed each abusive event). Reviewing the reasons you left will help remind you of how that life really was. Before you decide to return, you need to be sure you will not be stepping back into the same old abusive relationship.

Abuse is an extremely difficult pattern to break. Unless your ex-abuser is genuinely participating in ongoing long-term therapy, specifically designed to deal with people with abusive natures, the abuse *will* resurface. His participation in anger management classes or counseling will not truly make a difference. Your abuser most likely did not have an anger management problem. He did not blow up at work or get into physical fights with his friends. He carefully and thoughtfully chose how to control and abuse you. This is very different than someone with a general anger management problem (see the next section, "Treatment for the Abuser").

Rarely does the abuse end on its own. Even with effective treatment, abusers need time and a deep commitment to change. Unfortunately, most abusers aren't able to break the cycle and they repeat the abuse with partner after partner or with the same partner if they return.

Treatment for the Abuser

Very specific treatment has been developed for abusers. *Couples therapy* (sometimes referred to as marriage counseling) is *never* recommended and can actually be dangerous for a couple with one controlling and abusive partner. Sitting next to an abuser, the victim often feels intimidated and afraid to be honest with the counselor about the real problems in the relationship. Frequently this may cause the therapist to be unaware of the seriousness of the abuse or, at times, unknowingly side with the abuser. If the victim dares to mention the abuse, the abuse may worsen after the session. Therefore, couples therapy can escalate the abuser's power and control and create conditions that result in more frequent and escalating abuse.

Most professionals agree that the only effective treatment for abusers is what is known as *batterers' intervention groups*. These groups (designed primarily for male abusers) force abusers to examine their belief systems about women and relationships and to face head-on their violent behavior as well as the roots of their violence. However, for an abuser simply to begin a batterers' intervention group is not enough. An abuser must *complete* the entire treatment program, which typically takes up to a year. Even then, no one can guarantee that the abuse will not resurface, especially with the person who was the target of the abuse. Even with the best treatment, your abuser may return to controlling, abusive, or violent behaviors.

Therefore, if your ex-partner seeks treatment or seems to be getting better, you must be very careful and vigilant to be sure this is true. As you may well know, abusers are experts in subtle forms of manipulation and deception. Their abusive tendencies may not be gone at all. Instead, they may just find new techniques for concealing them. If you think your abuser has changed and you are considering going back, look for the most subtle signs that this is untrue. He may not be physically violent at first, but may rely on less obvious abusive tactics. Instead of throwing objects or striking you, he might just make a fist. You know what that fist means, and falling right into old patterns of fear and control, you do exactly what he wants. That same sickening knot in your gut comes back.

If alcohol or other drug use by your partner was part of the abuse in any way, this is another factor for you to consider. As we have said elsewhere in this book, **alcohol or other drugs do not *cause* relationship abuse or violence**, but they can help the abuser to "justify" it. Don't forget, abusers often try to excuse their behavior by blaming it on alcohol or other drugs. If your abuser claims to have stopped using alcohol or other drugs, and now is sober and that his abusive tendencies are gone, be cautious. Stopping the alcohol or other drugs does not end abuse.

Finally, listen to your gut and heart. If your interactions with your abuser produce the slightest decrease in your self-esteem, your sense of independence, or your feelings of safety, be extra cautious in deciding to return to that relationship.

Remember How Far You've Come

If you are thinking about going back to your abuser, what are some signs that you might be tempted to return to that relationship? Just as you need to go back with a full awareness of your partner's potential behavior, you may also benefit from looking at how you've changed since leaving. This will help you decide whether going back is worth the possibility of losing all that you have gained during your healing process. It will also help you determine the personal strengths and characteristics you will need to be able to return to that relationship as safely as possible.

Do you feel you would be able this time to stand up to the possibility of abusive behaviors should they happen again? Why? What is different about you now? If you ever consider going back be sure that your self-esteem, self-confidence, sense of personal security, and inner strength are powerful enough to allow you to escape the relationship again when the abuse returns.

How have you dealt with your hurt, anger, fear, and other emotions? Walking back into any relationship in which you have unresolved negative feelings might be setting yourself up for a difficult time. Most likely, if those unresolved feelings failed to heal while you were apart, they certainly will not heal when you are back in the relationship. If you are considering going back, you should be sure you perceive yourself as a confident, self-assured person who knows how much she deserves and will not settle for less.

If you have been struggling with an alcohol or other drug problem, you may want to consider this before returning to your former partner. If you return, you will need all your mental and physical faculties at their sharpest—you will need to be fully tuned in to your surroundings. Alcohol and other drugs helped you to cope in an abusive relationship; however, they also may make it more difficult for you to see all the subtle danger signs of your partner's abusive behavior and the reality of the relationship itself.

As we have stressed, in the end, only you can decide if it is in your best interest to return to that previously abusive relationship. You may want to talk your decision over with a trusted friend, family member, crisis center advocate, or therapist. Choose someone who will help you consider all sides of the issue and be honest with you about their insights, but not try to control your decision.

If very specific factors such as finances, living conditions, assistance with the children, or loneliness are making you feel that you have no choice but to go back, remember that you *always* have a choice. Explore every other possible option first. Talking over your options can help you find alternatives to going back.

Deciding Not to Go Back

If you decide not to go back, do not waste your time worrying about why you ever considered it. Feeling tempted to return to your abuser is a common and normal stage in the healing process. You are not weak or psychologically fragile.

When thoughts of returning appear, and they may from time to time, get out your lists of pros and cons. Remind yourself it's OK to remember and miss the good parts, but be sure you don't overlook the negatives.

Seek the support of friends. Tell them how they can help when you are in one of your "going back" phases. If it helps for them to remind you of all the reasons you left, ask them to do that. If you simply need them to listen, tell them that too.

Also, you could try reversing the roles. Look at yourself from another angle. What if someone you care deeply about was in the same situation? Imagine how you would feel if your best friend or family member managed to escape an abusive relationship such as yours and is now considering whether to go back. What would you think? What advice would you give? Would you suggest that going back? This imaginary "shoe-on-the-other-person's-foot" scenario may help you have more confidence in your decision. Whatever you choose to do, make sure your decisions are based on what is in *your* best interests. You deserve to have a loving, respectful, and safe intimate relationship.

If You Decide to Go Back

If you decide to return to your ex-partner, be sure to do so with your eyes wide open. Know ahead of time, no matter what is said or promised, most abusers usually, sooner or later, return to their old abusive ways. You may want to make the completion of a full batterers' intervention program a requirement for any discussion of reconciliation. If your ex becomes desperate and manipulative in his desire to get you back, be prepared for lying about any participation in such a program. Therefore, you need to arrange for your ex to sign a release of information so the therapist who facilitates the batterers' group may report your ex's attendance and progress to you directly.

If you are considering returning, establish your requirements and limits *now*. Decide what you must have from a relationship and what you will not accept—and stick to it. Drawing these lines early should help you take quick action to protect yourself if the relationship deteriorates into abuse and violence again.

Make an action plan. With a plan in place, you will be more likely to stay safely out of danger if you feel his abusive behaviors surfacing.

Be sure to keep close tabs on how you are feeling. Look for indicators of depression and any decrease in your self-esteem (see Chapter 9, "Signs of Unfinished Healing"). If you begin to feel these familiar responses, think of them as warnings of possible trouble ahead.

If you decide to go back, think about how you will deal with others in your life. Having an effective support network and people close to you whom you trust will be vitally important. Even if they do not agree with your decision, let them know you honestly feel it is the right one, you have considered it carefully, and you will continue to need them in your life.

Some of the most supportive people in your life may feel very frightened for your well-being, feel you are making the wrong decision, or even feel betrayed after they tried to help you. You may find them backing away from you. Try to keep the lines of communication open with them. Do not allow yourself to become isolated and totally dependent on your abusive partner once again.

Considering Your Options

When you are trying to decide whether to go back to an abusive relationship, some specific guidelines can be helpful. The following charts will help you look at various aspects of your relationship.

On the first chart, for each personality characteristic or behavior mark where you believe your ex-partner would have fallen on each dimension of the scale when you were together. On the second version of the chart mark where you believe your ex would fall today if you were to get back together.

When You Were Together

Trusting	— — — — — — — — — —	Suspicious
Respectful	— — — — — — — — — —	Humiliating
Predictable	— — — — — — — — — —	Unpredictable
Liberating	— — — — — — — — — —	Possessive
Equal	— — — — — — — — — —	Controlling
Secure	— — — — — — — — — —	Jealous
Good parent	— — — — — — — — — —	Abusive parent
Dependable	— — — — — — — — — —	Undependable
Stable	— — — — — — — — — —	Unstable
Empowering	— — — — — — — — — —	Demeaning
Willing to change	— — — — — — — — — —	Denies any problem exists
Unlikely to be violent	— — — — — — — — — —	Likely to be violent

Now, mark where you believe your ex-partner would fall on each dimension if you were to return to that relationship.

If You Return Now

Trusting	— — — — — — — — — —	Suspicious
Respectful	— — — — — — — — — —	Humiliating
Predictable	— — — — — — — — — —	Unpredictable
Liberating	— — — — — — — — — —	Possessive
Equal	— — — — — — — — — —	Controlling
Secure	— — — — — — — — — —	Jealous
Good parent	— — — — — — — — — —	Abusive parent
Dependable	— — — — — — — — — —	Undependable
Stable	— — — — — — — — — —	Unstable
Empowering	— — — — — — — — — —	Demeaning
Willing to change	— — — — — — — — — —	Denies any problem exists
Unlikely to be violent	— — — — — — — — — —	Likely to be violent

This information, combined with your responses to the *Self-Exploration* exercise in Chapter 1 ("Were You in an Abusive Relationship?"), will provide a foundation for helping you to make the right decision about returning to your abuser.

16

Is Your Abuser Still in Your Life?

Myth: Once you leave an abusive relationship, you are free from any interactions with your abuser.

Myth: Following an abusive relationship you have control over all contacts with your ex-partner.

Myth: Now that you are out, your abuser no longer has the power to exert any control over you.

No matter how much you would like to exclude your ex-partner from your life, it is not always possible to do so. Your abuser may continue to be a part of your current life in many ways and contact may be unavoidable, especially if you have children together. Therefore, developing effective strategies to deal with your ex is a vital component in your healing process.

If You Are Fearful of Contact

As mentioned throughout this book, just because you escape an abusive relationship, the danger does not always go away and many times it becomes worse. If you have reason to be fearful of your abuser, and your abuser knows where you work or live, it becomes even more imperative that you reexamine your personal safety needs. Review Chapter 2—"Are You Out of Danger Now?"—and take all necessary steps to maximize your safety.

If your ex attempts any contact with you while a restraining order is in force, call the police immediately. Don't wait for the situation to get out of hand. The easiest way to keep your abuser out of your life is to demonstrate clearly that you will not be controlled again. This time, *you* are the one in control of your life. Every situation is unique, but if possible, it is wise for you to avoid ever initiating any contact. If you do, or if you respond to your ex's overtures in any way, you may be allowing a "foot in the door," and most abusers are masters of squeezing through that crack.

Contact at Work or in the Community

If you and your abuser are still living in the same community, you may have no choice about seeing each other. If you work in the same location, you may have to interact on a frequent or even daily basis. Getting on with your life might be a bit more difficult under these conditions.

Even if you are unable to avoid contact, you have every right to insist that any talking or interacting happen on your terms. If your ex refuses to comply with your boundaries, you may need to consider a restraining order (see Chapter 12, "Practical Considerations").

Indirect Contact through Others

Your abuser may reappear in your life through your family and friends. Remember how charming others thought your ex-partner was? Abusers are masters at fooling others into thinking they are wonderful partners. When survivors leave, abusers often become desperate to get them back. This may make abusers more dangerous than ever before. Your ex may try anything and everything to recapture you, including using the people who are still in your life.

Abusers often maintain contact with your family and friends, working to convince them that nothing bad will ever happen again; to win their approval; and enlist their help. Abusers will say that they have changed, the children need them, they have been getting help, and will do anything for another chance. On the other hand, an abuser's tactics may include intimidating or bullying your intimate family members.

You might have believed your ex about these things. Your loved ones may feel the same. This will be particularly true if they know you are struggling and having a difficult time on your own. They will be looking for a reconciliation, a "storybook" ending. In their desire to make you happy, they may be fooled by your abuser's overtures.

You can be understanding but firm with your friends and family. Let them know you appreciate how much they care. Let them know that you are very aware of how convincing your abuser can seem. Then, try to help them see the deception and why you are choosing never to return to an abusive partner. If they are not able or willing to see these truths, you may need to give careful consideration to whether and how much they should be part of your new life (see Chapter 11, "The Reactions of Others").

Unwanted Contacts with Your Ex's "Camp"

You may also find that your abuser's family and friends will contact *you*. They will be working to convince you that your ex is sorry and is really a great person. You need to be prepared to respond effectively and firmly to these contacts.

Those who see or talk to your ex on an ongoing basis probably do not fully understand what happened in your relationship. At this point, trying to enlighten them will probably be futile. If they contact you, the best approach is to tell them in very clear language how you feel and what you do and do not want. Resist arguing with them. Do not try to reason with them. Just let them know your limits.

Keep in mind that whatever you tell them will be passed along to your ex-partner. So, be careful about how much you say. You do not need to explain or defend your decisions to anyone. You simply need to inform them of what you want and expect, not only from your abuser, but from them as well. If you want no further contact with them, tell them so. Again, be clear and firm.

Contact through the Children

One of the most common reasons that a survivor must have contact with her ex-partner involves children. If you and your ex-partner had children together, visitation rights may be required (see Chapter 10, "What About the Children?"). Another possibility is that you may have been forced to leave your children with your abuser when you escaped. Seeing your children now may necessitate seeing your abuser as well.

If your ex-partner has visitation rights, it will be important for you to plan visits that will be as safe as possible for you and your children. Some cities and towns provide *visitation centers*, which allow visits between parents and children in safe, supervised settings. Contact your local sexual assault and domestic violence crisis center for information about visitation centers in your area. Be sure to read Chapter 10—"What About the Children?"—for additional information on visitation safety.

If your area does not have a visitation center, try to find the safest way possible for visits with the children. Try to find a safe, public place to exchange the children. If it would make you feel better, ask a trusted adult to come with you for the exchange. If your abuser is allowed to pick up the children at your home, consider having a friend or family member present or allow that person to make the exchange instead of you.

What the Children Tell You

Even if you do not have direct contact, you may hear about your ex-partner. From a distance, your abuser can attempt to influence and control you through your children. Your ex may plant stories and comments, knowing the children will convey them to you. If your children see your abuser, they're bound to tell you about their visits. As painful as that may be for you, it will be more painful to forbid your kids to talk about your ex-partner. That puts *them* in the middle, which may be exactly what your ex wants. It is important for you to anticipate manipulative behaviors by your ex, including using the children as "weapons." The more prepared you are for these indirect maneuvers, the easier it will be for you to deal with them when they occur.

You may believe your abuser would never hurt your children, because all the abuse was directed at you. Sadly, after the relationship ends, an abuser may employ new tactics to control you, including abusive acts directed at your children.

You may need to be extremely cautious about your children's safety. If your ex-partner has contact with your children through a visitation center, be sure you clearly understand the rules of that center. They will have a very strict set of regulations that must be obeyed for the visits. These rules will prohibit all violence or threats of violence toward you or your children. They will also prevent your abuser from determining through the children where you are living or gaining access to you in any way. The trained staff should help ensure that the children cannot be used in any way to hurt you further.

When the center's rules are broken, be sure to contact someone at the center immediately. Do not pass it off as a small transgression and let it go. When abusers get away with one infraction, they will continue to push the limits. Remember, your ex wants to control your life and you need to undermine that effort at every possible turn.

Lying to the Children

Your abuser might try to control you by lying to the children, to convince them that *you* are the reason the family is not together, or that you were the one who was cruel. Abusers may fabricate lies designed to turn the children against you. Hearing your children repeat these lies can have a profound emotional effect on you. Your children may frame the lies as questions to you or they may repeat them as statements of "fact." If they are posed as questions, try to respond without anger and resist your temptation to inhibit their desire for answers. If you are not able to respond calmly, just tell them you will talk to them about it later. Be sure to keep that promise.

When you talk with your children, remember that they are being used and placed in the middle by your abuser. They are trying to understand a very confusing situation. They may love your ex-partner, who may have told them that you hurt him. In asking you about it, they are trusting you to help them understand. Try to be reassuring and nonaccusatory. Be willing to listen as they tell you how hurt and upset your ex feels. Acknowledge how unsettling it must be for them to hear this. You also need to tell them that you have no choice. You cannot all live together anymore. And even though they may not understand it right now, you cannot do anything to make your former partner feel better.

Encourage them to come to you whenever they are confused or have questions. Let them know you will always love them no matter what they say or ask. Make sure they know they are not to blame for what happened between you and your abuser.

Another way your abuser can control you is by trying to alter the children's memory of what actually happened. Your ex might tell them *you* were the one who was abusive. Your ex will probably say he never hurt you or them, or the abuse was only because of love. Your abuser might try to brainwash them. You know firsthand how good abusers are at brainwashing others.

Your former partner might tell the children you will be together again as a family one day, and if only you would give in, you could all be happy. Your abuser might try anything to turn the children against you or to use them to regain control over you. Again, try to talk gently and rationally with your children about the reality of the situation without directly accusing your ex of lying.

Using the Children to Control Your Activities

Another way your former abuser might exert control over you is by manipulating your schedule through the children by playing mind games about when, where, and how they will get to see each other. Your ex might try to inconvenience you as much as possible to accommodate visitation privileges with the children, or even use the children as a weapon, threatening to refuse to see them at all if you don't behave in certain ways.

Recognize these games as attempts to control you again. If you feel that your abuser's behaviors are becoming too difficult or unhealthy for your children, you have to ask yourself whether they should see your ex at all. And if your abuser threatens to cut off all contact with the children to try to make you do or say something, then eliminating such contact just might be the best action to take.

Refusing to Be Controlled

Survivors often feel extremely frustrated when their former abusers manage to stay in their lives. You needed incredible courage and energy to leave. Now it may feel like you will never get rid of your ex. You need to decide now what role, if any, you will allow your abuser to play in your life. If you decide that no role at all is what you want, try not to allow any contact, directly or indirectly, to exert any control over you. If you cannot avoid contact with your ex-partner, work on finding strategies to make it as emotionally easy for yourself as possible. If you cannot find the strength within yourself for this, enlist the help of police, friends, family, or a counselor. Seeking help is not a sign of weakness. After all, you are dealing with a very difficult situation and a dangerous person.

Planning Ahead for Contact

Part I

What will you do if or when your abuser confronts you? It's a good idea to think about and plan for it now, so when it happens, you will be as prepared and in control as possible. The exercise below contains situations in which you may have contact with your ex-partner. Check all the ones you either know or think could apply to you. Then, in the space provided, indicate your best and most effective courses of action in that situation. You can always come back to this exercise and change your plans as needed.

Contacituation	Action Plan
_____ My abuser shows up where I work	
_____ I run into my abuser in a public place	
_____ My abuser comes to my home	
_____ Our paths cross at a family function	
_____ We see each other at work or school	
_____ My abuser is at my friend's house when I come to visit	
_____ We are both at the same restaurant	
_____ Other possible contact situations (list) _____ _____ _____	

Part II: The Children

As mentioned earlier, for some survivors, the most frequent contact with their former abuser is through the children. If this applies to you, this exercise is designed to help you think ahead about how you will handle those situations. Again, check all of the scenarios that could apply to you. For each of the possible scenarios listed below, write down some ideas for what you might say to your children if these issues arise.

Issue with Child	Your Possible Responses
_____ Your abuser tells the children the abuse was all your fault	
_____ Your abuser tells the children that you are preventing them from being a happy family again	
_____ Your abuser agrees to see the children at specific times and then fails to show up	
_____ Your abuser tells the children you are preventing them from having more time together	
_____ Other possible contact situations (list) _____ _____ _____	

Remember, when an abuser is still in your life, you cannot predict what might happen. Thinking about potentially difficult situations and planning ahead as best you can is one of your best defenses against unexpected and potentially dangerous contact.

17

Loving Again

Myth: Survivors of abusive relationships are doomed to repeat the cycle.

Myth: Surviving an abusive relationship makes you an expert in predicting whether your next potential partner has controlling or violent tendencies.

Myth: Most survivors are never again able to find a truly intimate, loving relationship.

As a survivor of an abusive relationship, you may find it very difficult to allow intimacy into your life again. You are no longer able to enter into a new relationship with innocence and trust. You now carry with you the knowledge, and more important, the wisdom, of how love can go terribly wrong. Your experience of abuse means you may enter any new relationship with great caution. This is perfectly normal and very smart.

Are You Doomed to Repeat the Past?

Just because you survived an abusive relationship does not, by any means, suggest that you will have to endure others. If anything, you will be better prepared to see the warning signs of a future partner's potential for controlling and abusive behavior. You can use what you have learned (the hard way) to recognize abusive signals that a potential partner may exhibit.

Hopefully, by now you should have no doubt in your mind that you were not to blame for your abusive relationship. You weren't stupid or blind or too trusting. Abusers are expert at concealing their abusive and violent nature. You had no way of seeing through the external charm and attractiveness. Now that you have experienced and survived your terrible ordeal, you can look back on your relationship and become more aware of the signs that predicted the abuse.

What Is a Healthy Relationship?

No two people want exactly the same qualities in an intimate relationship. Characteristics that are very significant to you may be less important to someone else. There are, however, some key elements of healthy relationships that all of us deserve with our intimate partners.

Equality is very important. Equality doesn't imply that you and your partner are the same. It doesn't mean you both should share all the same activities such as fixing the car, doing the dishes, paying the bills, planting the garden. It means there is a sense of balance in your relationship that is mutually agreed upon. This applies to all activities from chores and work to an equal share in all family decisions.

Everyone deserves *respect* from an intimate partner. Respect should permeate all aspects of your relationship. It's not enough to respect someone simply because of physical appearance, cooking abilities, or musical talent. You deserve to be respected for *who you are as a person*, positive characteristics, flaws, and all.

Trust is another crucial ingredient in all healthy relationships. It is essential to know you can rely on your partner. This means that your new partner should be honest and consistent. You should never have to question the validity of what an intimate partner is telling you. Above all else, you should be able to trust that there will never be any abuse or violence.

What Do You Want in an Intimate Relationship?

Only you can determine who is the right partner for you, who has the qualities to make you content and happy. However, establishing these criteria may be easier said than done. But it's essential for you to be clear about what you want in a relationship, and to remind yourself of your requirements each time a new potential partner enters your life. This chapter and the *Self-Exploration* exercise at the end, "What to Look For and What to Avoid," are designed to help you with this task.

Warning Signs of Abuse

When you first met your ex-partner, you probably weren't looking for warning signs of abuse. You weren't keeping your eyes wide open for words or actions that might offer clues of what was to come. Mentally recording language, gestures, and actions that tied your stomach into a knot wasn't foremost in your mind.

Some abusers are so skilled at hiding their true selves that no one, no matter how informed and experienced, would be able to predict that they are capable of such abusive and violent actions. Other abusers may give off such subtle signs that only someone trained to know what to look for could detect them.

So, what are some of the subtle signs that you should keep on your abuse radar screen? Indicators fall into two categories: subtle negative precursors of abuse and, paradoxically, even more obvious signs in the form of seemingly wonderful, charming behaviors that feel beyond belief or "too good to be true."

Too Much of a Good Thing

Abusers can appear to be gracious, giving, loving, and devoted partners. From the moment you meet, they are working overtime to charm, impress, and entice you into a relationship. There is no end to how wonderful they appear while courting you. But how can you tell if a potential mate is simply the virtuous, caring person you are looking for or a wolf in sheep's clothing?

It's wonderful to be placed on a pedestal, and that's what everyone feels they want from an intimate partner. Unfortunately, being up on that pedestal can also be a warning sign. When you get placed on a pedestal, you are transformed into the other's ideal image of a lover, without any flaws, who will always do and be exactly what is expected of you. It's your partner's pedestal, not yours, and it can be dangerous up there.

You Are "Perfect"

No one is perfect. And when your partner says how perfect you are, this sets up an expectation of an impossible standard to meet. If a potential partner seems to be re-creating you in such an image, it's important to determine what this really means. If it is just a way of saying you are wonderful and an expression of real, unconditional love, that is probably a positive sign. But if your partner truly thinks of you as *perfect*, that's potentially dangerous.

If you are concerned that your partner is expecting perfection, make sure to avoid hiding your imperfections. If you are not always the most punctual person, do not go overboard to be consistently on time. If you are not the best housekeeper in the world, let your partner see your home as it usually is: less than immaculate. *Be yourself.*

If you fail to live up to your partner's image of you, and your imperfections are not met with anger, or criticisms, you may have less reason to be concerned. However, if a potential partner becomes annoyed, makes judgmental comments or jokes, or attempts to blame you for not meeting certain "expectations," red flags and sirens should go off in your head.

Too Persistent

Another seductive characteristic that is often a danger sign of an abuser is extreme persistence. If you are hesitant to become involved, but a potential partner refuses to take no for an answer, be alert. It's one thing for someone to be interested in you, but to pursue you nonstop, even when you are withdrawing and asking for space, is a very disturbing sign.

This overenthusiasm may also be evident in a desire to move the relationship forward too quickly. If you hear expressions of great desire for a commitment (exclusivity, living together, marriage) soon after meeting, that's a good reason to be alarmed. Consider why someone would want or need a relationship to proceed at such a frantic pace. Is it love, or is it an intense jealousy, insecurity, or a desire for control already showing?

If the speed of your partner's desire for commitment makes you uncomfortable, see what happens if you step on the brakes. If it's true and healthy love, you should feel that your desires and needs are being respected. If you say you want to slow things down, that desire should be valued. You should feel able to exert control at this point. This means your partner should agree to take it as slowly as you want without pressuring you to pick up the pace or ridiculing you about going too slowly.

Monopolizing

Pay attention to the amount of time a potential partner wants to spend with you. In any new relationship partners usually express a desire to get to know the other person and the excitement of exploring someone new runs high. So how can you tell the difference between a genuine desire for togetherness and early attempts to control you?

At the beginning of a new relationship, you may want to consciously limit your time together to specific, planned activities. This sets clear limits. If your potential partner frequently shows up unannounced, you should be cautious. Say you prefer to arrange and plan your time together. If you are confronted at your job, explain that it is not a good time or place for you to meet. If you feel your wishes in this regard are ignored, problems are looming on the horizon.

If a potential partner expresses a desire to spend every evening and weekend together and calls you frequently in between, make it clear that you are not yet ready to become involved with anyone to that extent. Suggest that you see each other only a couple of nights per week. Be firm that you have plans on other evenings and on the weekend and you need some time to yourself. Pay attention to how this is received and take those reactions into consideration. If you feel discounted or ignored, the control is beginning.

Jealousy

If a new partner shows signs of jealousy early, before you are even a couple, this indicates a problem. If you are sensing that possessiveness or expressions of ownership are escalating as the relationship continues, be watchful. If a potential partner becomes jealous without a reason, that should be a red flag. If the jealousy is out of proportion with your innocent interactions with other people, that, too, is a reason for concern. Such jealousy is not the result of an intense attraction to you or how desirable you may be to others. As flattering as that may feel, you need to recognize that excessive jealousy is about insecurity and your partner's need to control you. It is *not* about love and caring.

Isolating You

Isolating you from other people in your life is a very disturbing indication of future danger. If your partner always wants to be alone with you and resists spending time with your family and friends, this may be the beginning of future attempts to isolate you. Another sign of this control tactic is a tendency to manipulate you into canceling plans with others so that the two of you can be alone. Again, it may sound romantic, but a pattern of this behavior is not romantic, it's dangerous.

One way to try to protect yourself from future abusive relationships is to be sure to maintain friends and activities of your own. Never allow a potential partner to attempt to dictate whom you may or may not see, where you may or may not go, or what you may or may not do in your own life.

"It's-Not-All-That-Bad" Thinking

It's very important to keep an eye on behaviors that annoy you but don't yet feel like true warning signs. Someone without your experience of abuse might easily dismiss them. Here are some examples.

- As we discussed earlier, excessive jealousy may begin with the feeling that you are being monitored all the time. It is a worrisome sign if your partner calls you too frequently at home or at work or makes a habit of questioning you about your whereabouts or whom you were with at a specific time. An abuser may find creative excuses for the persistent phone calls and questions, or may just chalk them up to missing you so intensely. But you know better.

- Be very cautious if you find that your partner is following you. Although there may not be any overt contact, you may see a familiar car driving by your home or workplace. When you are out with your friends, your partner may "coincidentally" show up. All of these are signs of a jealous and controlling nature that are clear warnings.

- Be alert if your partner tries to make most of the decisions in your relationship, such as where you will go together, whom you will visit as a couple, what activities you will share. If your desires differ, do yours always seem to take second place? Do you feel subtly discounted and disparaged when you try to choose activities to do together? These are also clear indicators of controlling tendencies.

- Another sign of a need to dominate you involves jokes and subtle put-downs about you and issues that are important to you. This may take the form of demeaning teasing or joking about your personal idiosyncrasies such as being occasionally late, keeping a somewhat messy home, or driving cautiously. These warning signs may be more noticeable if they involve teasing and joking about you in the presence of others.

If you are unsure whether these warning behaviors indicate trouble ahead, put them to the test. Confront the behaviors. Refuse to accept them. See if your partner hears you and agrees to the changes you desire and keeps those agreements. *You do not need to rush into any relationship.* Trusting someone may take time, but it will be worth the wait to find someone who is truly right and healthy for you.

Looking Inside Yourself

How do you know if you are ready for a new relationship? Along with your careful analysis of a potential new relationship, you will find it helpful to evaluate your *own* readiness to become romantically involved.

What does it mean to be "ready" for a new intimate relationship? In a general sense, it means feeling psychologically and emotionally fit to begin a new, loving partnership. Because no one is without insecurities or faults, what can you look for as indicators of your readiness?

Being ready to have an intimate partner in your life implies that you honestly feel good about *yourself*. Do you believe you deserve a trusting, loving, respectful, abuse-free relationship? Are you confident that you can be a caring, loving partner for someone? In other words, is your self-esteem strong enough for you to enter a relationship as an *equal* partner? This sense of yourself as someone who has a fundamental right to equality in a relationship is a necessary ingredient for the success of any future healthy relationship.

Another indicator of your readiness for a new relationship is how well you have dealt with the difficult issues in your life following the abuse, such as depression, fear, trusting others, anger, and problems with alcohol or other drugs. After what you've been through, it would be unfair to yourself (and to your partner) to begin a new relationship angry, depressed, or addicted. Any one or more of these will only cause you to feel bad about yourself and unworthy of your partner. If there is a possibility of a new intimate partner in your life, you both should be willing to take it slowly and wait until you feel that you are whole again and truly ready for the give-and-take a successful relationship requires.

New relationships can be exciting and exhilarating, but they can also be stressful. Any life change, good or bad, brings with it some degree of stress. Before you begin a new partnership, be sure that the other sources of stress in your life are reasonably manageable. The last thing you want is to start a new relationship feeling totally overwhelmed by other issues. All good relationships take time, energy, and work.

If your former partner sexually assaulted you, you may need to work through some of that trauma before being intimate with a new partner. You may have been able to do this on your own, or you may need the assistance of a counselor. Either way, when you become intimate with your next partner, the prospect of the intimacy and the experience itself should feel loving and pleasurable for you. It should not cause you to feel afraid, ashamed, or overwhelmed.

For some survivors, beginning a new relationship can be a frightening venture given the trauma they have experienced. Don't allow someone to talk you into something before you are ready. When the time is right, you will be able to stand your ground and take the time you need to explore a new partner and establish a new, healthy relationship.

A New Relationship, a New Beginning

At some point, you will begin to look forward to a new, healthy intimate relationship. At the same time, you may continue to feel some very real fear about taking that risk. You have countless valid reasons for your fear and hesitation. Probably, what you fear more than anything else is the chance that you will become involved with another abusive person. Although that fear is perfectly normal, if you approach new relationships with caution and the wisdom that comes from experience, your fear will give way to a healthy connection with a loving partner. This will not happen overnight, but it *will* come with time.

The ease with which you are able to complete this exercise may offer you some clues about your readiness for a new relationship.

A. List five qualities you will absolutely require in a new partner (such as "respect for my feelings" or "gentleness"). These are nonnegotiable.

Qualities I will require:

1. _____

2. _____

3. _____

4. _____

5. _____

B. List five qualities you will positively avoid in a new partner (such as being overly judgmental of you or coming on too strong too fast). These are unacceptable.

Qualities I will not accept:

1. _____

2. _____

3. _____

4. _____

5. _____

C. List five "red flags" that you feel would be your best personal indicators that you should either be extra careful of a new relationship, or get out of it entirely (such as jealousy, isolating you from others).

"My red flags" for potential abuse:

1. _____

2. _____

3. _____

4. _____

5. _____

Resources

We have included the following resources to help you obtain more information about relationship abuse and domestic violence and to assist you in finding the support you need in your ongoing process of healing.

- **National Domestic Violence Hotline, U.S.** Department of Justice, Violence Against Women Office
  Counseling, information and referrals across the country.
  1-800-799-SAFE (7233)
  1-800-787-3224 (TTY)
  www.thehotline.org
- **Rape, Abuse & Incest National Network (RAINN)**
  800-656-HOPE (4673)
  www.rainn.org
- **National Coalition Against Domestic Violence**
  303-839-1852
  www.ncadv.org
- **American Bar Association Commission on Domestic Violence**
  www.abanet.org/domviol

- **National Network to End Domestic Violence**
  Does not work directly with survivors but provides
  information and links to many resources you can contact them
  through their Web site.
  https://nnedv.org
- **National Center for Victims of Crime**
  855-4-VICTIM
  http://victimsofcrime.org
- **National Center on Domestic and Sexual Violence**
  www.ncdsv.org
- **National Gay and Lesbian Task Force**
  Washington, DC: 202-393-5177
  New York, NY: 212-604-9830
  Cambridge, MA: 617-492-6393
  Miami Beach, FL: 305-571-1924
  Minneapolis, MN: 612-821-4397
  www.thetaskforce.org
- **Feminist Majority Foundation's Domestic Violence
  Information Center**
  Phone numbers included by state.
  www.feminist.org/911/crisis.html
- **SAMSHA**, Substance Abuse and Mental Health Services
  Administration
  1-800-662-HELP (4357)
  www.samhsa.gov/find-help/national-helpline

Index

Page numbers in *italics* denote figures.